Synopsis of Jewish History

H. A. Henry

Alpha Editions

This edition published in 2024

ISBN : 9789366383118

Design and Setting By
Alpha Editions
www.alphaedis.com
Email - info@alphaedis.com

As per information held with us this book is in Public Domain.
This book is a reproduction of an important historical work. Alpha Editions uses the best technology to reproduce historical work in the same manner it was first published to preserve its original nature. Any marks or number seen are left intentionally to preserve its true form.

Contents

PREFACE. ....- 1 -

CHAPTER I. ....- 2 -

CHAPTER II. ....- 5 -

CHAPTER III. ....- 10 -

CHAPTER IV. ....- 17 -

CHAPTER V. ....- 20 -

CHAPTER VI. ....- 23 -

CHAPTER VII. ....- 27 -

CHAPTER VIII. ....- 31 -

CHAPTER IX. ....- 40 -

CHAPTER X. ....- 49 -

Part Second. ....- 57 -

CHAPTER I. ....- 59 -

CHAPTER II. ....- 60 -

CHAPTER III. ....- 62 -

CHAPTER IV. ....- 64 -

CHAPTER V.	- 66 -
CHAPTER VI.	- 67 -
CHAPTER VII.	- 68 -
CHAPTER VIII.	- 69 -
CHAPTER IX.	- 71 -
CHAPTER X.	- 74 -
CHAPTER XI.	- 79 -
CHAPTER XII.	- 82 -
CHAPTER XIII.	- 92 -
CHAPTER XIV.	- 94 -

PREFACE.

The design and purpose of this little production will, at a cursory glance, be self-evident, so that a formal preface seems scarcely necessary. We have endeavored to furnish a synopsis of useful information, selected from the history and teachings of the chosen people of God, in such a manner as to suit the capacity of all readers, since it is free from all sectarian bias, and therefore may prove useful to all denominations.

This work consists of two parts. The first part contains a synopsis of Jewish history, commencing with the return of the Jews from the Babylonish captivity, down to the days of Herod the Great. The second division of the work contains an account of the several sects which sprang up among the Jews before and after the days of the Maccabees. We have also given a succinct description of the origin and introduction of Prayer, of the synagogues and schools, of the Ureem and Thumeem, of the Mishna or Oral Law, of the Gemara or Completion, usually styled the Talmud, together with some additional remarks in the last two chapters under the head of appendix.

Should this unassuming little composition lead the reader to seek a more extended information on the subjects treated, we shall feel ourselves happy in having been the means of thus exciting the curiosity of those who desire to peep a little further into the vast field of sacred literature, and deem our compensation to be fully realized.

We have compiled in some instances from the writings of others. In many cases we have also thought for ourselves; but at the same time, we have embraced the advantages afforded by the writings of others, so far as we thought them suitable for the undertaking.

In conclusion, we send this work out to the world, such as it is, aware of its many deficiencies; trusting, at the same time, that whatever errors may have crept therein will be pointed out by kind friends, in order to a rectification of the same.

SAN FRANCISCO, February, 1859—5619.

CHAPTER I.

Of the Return of the Jews from the Captivity of Babylon, and the Rebuilding of the City of Jerusalem and the Holy Temple.

In fulfilment of the prophecies of Jeremiah and the other prophets, Israel and Judah were carried into captivity by Nebuchadnezzar, king of Babylon, in the days of Zedekiah, the last king of Judah; and as predicted by the prophets of the Lord, the bondage continued during seventy years.

This banishment was inflicted as a just punishment on the people for their repeated misconduct and impiety towards the Gracious God, and for their direct opposition to the constant exhortations and unceasing warnings of the Almighty, through the medium of his inspired and holy prophets.

The seventy years of captivity being ended, God put it into the mind of Cyrus, king of Persia, again to restore Israel to their own land and possessions, thus fulfilling the prophecy of Isaiah, which was pronounced by him above one hundred years previously. Accordingly Cyrus permitted the Jews to return to Jerusalem and to rebuild the temple. He also restored to them the golden and silver vessels which were used for divine service in the former temple built by king Solomon.

Many of the people of the several tribes availed themselves of this opportunity to return to the land of their fathers—but so far as history informs us, it appears that the majority of those who returned to Jerusalem, consisted chiefly of the tribes of Judah and Benjamin, together with a number of Priests and Levites. And now it was for the first time, that they were all united under the title or name of Jews.

The people were led forth under the direction of Zerubbabel, the grandson of Jehoiachin, king of Judah, who became the governor of the land by a commission granted at the hands of king Cyrus; and Jeshua, the grandson of Seraiah, who was slain by Nebuchadnezzar, was installed high priest.

The people having returned to their own land, the first thing which occupied their attention was the rebuilding of the temple, for which purpose they set about making collections, both of money and materials, and gathering themselves together at Jerusalem, they set up the altar, and offered sacrifices thereon in gratitude to God for his goodness in thus restoring them to their own country and possessions.

When the foundation of the new temple was laid, great rejoicings took place among the people. Yet, many of those who had grown old in the captivity, and who still had the recollection of the glory and magnificence of the first temple, mourned and grieved for its loss, and very much despaired of the second temple ever approaching the first, in beauty, splendor, or holiness.

The building of the second temple was very much interrupted by the neighboring people, who manifested great enmity toward the Jews, and evinced much jealous feeling, when they saw them restored to their own country, and thus likely to recover their long lost national position in the world.

Yet, notwithstanding all the difficulties which presented themselves, and in spite of all the representations made by their enemies, the Jews were favored with great assistance from the court of Persia, in order to complete their noble undertaking. And then it was, that after a period of twenty years interrupted labor, the second temple rose on the very same spot on which the first noble fabric had adorned the happy days of the royal Solomon, the son of king David.

In the days of Darius Hystaspes, complaints were made by the enemies of the Jews, in order to prevent them from continuing the building of the temple. This prince, considering the interruption to be the result of the malicious insinuations of the Samaritans and their followers, instituted an inquiry, and it being found on record at Babylon that permission had been granted to the Jews by Cyrus to rebuild the temple at Jerusalem, Darius immediately gave orders that the work should be continued undisturbed. And in the sixth year of the reign of Darius, the second temple was completed, and dedicated for divine worship. Sacrifices were resumed, and offered upon the altar of the Lord as in former days. Great rejoicings prevailed, and the festival of Passover was in that year solemnized in great splendor, and with grateful feelings toward the God of their fathers.

Happy, however, as the people appeared to be in again beholding the house of God reared and dedicated to his holy worship, they still felt and saw the deficiency in the one, when compared with the other; for it must be observed, that in the second temple but few of the glories remained which had adorned the first temple, so renowned in history for its beauty, magnificence, and architectural delicacy and elegance.

The temple erected by king Solomon at Jerusalem, was built after the model of the tabernacle erected in the wilderness. This superb edifice was completed in about seven years. Its grandeur and magnificence excited the envy and the curiosity of all the surrounding nations.

The glory of this temple, however, did not consist in the magnitude of its dimensions alone. The main grandeur and excellency were in its ornaments, the workmanship being everywhere curiously and exquisitely wrought by the most expert workmen of the day. But still more admirable in this majestic building, were those extraordinary works of divine favor with which it was honored. These, indeed, were excellencies and beauties derived from a divine source only, distinguishing and exalting this sacred structure above all others of mortal invention.

The deficiencies thus complained of and regretted, were five in number, which formed the principal and most essential ornaments of the sacred edifice.

FIRST.—The ark of the covenant, and the mercy seat upon it; the cherubim of gold, and the two tables of stone, on which the decalogue was inscribed by the finger of God. These were all in their proper places in the first temple built by king Solomon. It is the generally received opinion among the learned men of the Jewish nation, that there was such an ark made, and that the copy of the five books of Moses, called the Pentateuch—as corrected and revised by the scribe Ezra—was deposited therein. Hence, it is in imitation of this, that in the present day, the Jews have in their synagogues throughout all the habitable globe wherever dispersed, the holy ark in which the scroll of the law called in Hebrew "Sepher Torah," book of the law, is deposited.

SECOND.—The Shechinah, divine presence manifested by a visible cloud of glory hovering over the mercy seat.

THIRD.—The Ureem and Thumeem. These were two sacred signs placed in the breast-plate of judgment worn by the high priest, who made use of these signs to consult the will of God, and to ask counsel of him on such momentous occasions touching the public interest of the nation at large. The first of these words signifies in the Hebrew, light; the second, perfection. Of these we shall have to speak more fully in the course of the work.

FOURTH.—The sacred fire which descended from on high upon the altar, to consume the daily sacrifices and burnt offerings brought in honor of the Lord God of hosts.

FIFTH.—The spirit of prophecy; for though the three last prophets, Haggai, Zachariah, and Malachi, lived during the time of the second temple, yet, after their death, the prophetic spirit ceased to exist any longer among the Jewish nation.

CHAPTER II.

Of the state of the Jews in the days of Ezra the Scribe.

Henceforward we are not to look on the Jews, free, rich and glorious, under the direction of Prophets and warlike Monarchs; they had been sold as slaves by their conquerors, and dispersed throughout all their vast and mighty Empires. Some few of the favored, eminent and worthy characters obtained posts of honor, who distinguished themselves in the discharge of those duties imposed on them in their several appointments. Of the great number of the people who had been carried into captivity, scarcely more than fifty thousand returned to Jerusalem, and those were principally of the poorer classes, who, it must be noticed, are in all ages the most religious. The richer portion of the nation remained behind—and, as proverbial with the Jews for their charity and fellow feeling, they raised among themselves a subscription sufficient to enable their brethren to proceed on their holy pilgrimage.

The proposal made to the Jews was, that they should be governed by their own laws; but as they became subject to Persia, and subsequently to Syria and Rome, their privileges, and even the exercise of their religion, greatly depended on the caprice of their several conquerors. Immediately on the publication of the edict, the Chief of the tribes of Judah and Benjamin assembled at Babylon, with the Priests and Levites; and as many who retained a love for their country and a zeal for the honor of their God, were disposed to return to that once happy land, and now came and signified their intention of returning. The wealthy portion, and many who formed connections with them, and were engaged in traffic, or had acquired places and employments, chose rather to stay and content themselves with raising a large contribution to supply their brethren with what they could spare of gold, silver, and other valuables for the Temple.

The book of Ezra informs us of the three great and pious men whom God raised up to assist the poor Jews, and gives us some particulars of their return to Jerusalem. Zerubbabel, who built the Temple and the Altar; Ezra, who reformed and re-established the sacred religion to its former standard, which, during the captivity had undergone many changes and innovations; as the people were not in a position at that time fully to observe it, as it was practised in the palmy days of their Fathers; and Nehemiah, who built the walls of the City, and ably assisted Ezra in his good work in introducing and ultimately effecting a great and solid improvement among the people. This book embraces a period of about one hundred and forty-six years, and the acts thereof were accomplished during the reigns of six successive Persian Monarchs, viz: Cyrus, Darius, Ahasuerus, Artaxerxes, Darius the second, and a second Artaxerxes. About eighty years after their establishment, Ezra obtained a full commission from Artaxerxes to succeed Zerubbabel, the present Viceroy, and return to Jerusalem, with as many of the nation as were willing to go with him; and there to regulate and reform all matters of State, and restore the worship of the true God among his people in the city of Jerusalem.

The high reputation of Ezra in the Court of Persia, may be imagined by the nature of the commission granted to him by the King, who addressed him as the Priest of the Law of the God of Heaven; and declared to him as his decree, that whosoever felt desirous to go up to Jerusalem were permitted to do so freely and safely; and furthermore, that they should take with them presents direct from the King himself, as a proof of his sanction and approbation. In the middle of March, about the year of the World 3540, Ezra set out on his journey, and pitched his tents on the banks of the river Ahavah, where he waited till his companions had assembled together, from whom he selected a number of Priests and Levites to assist him on the journey.

As soon as Ezra had collected about him a large body of people, he issued a proclamation for a general fast and days of thanksgiving, to implore the blessing and protection of God. He then proceeded on his journey, and arrived safely with all his company at Jerusalem in the middle of the month of July, being about four months after he had set out for Jerusalem.

Having arrived at Jerusalem, Ezra convened all the Elders of the people, before whom he laid open his Commission and had it publicly read to all the people. He then delivered up to the Treasury and the Priests, all the presents which had been made by the Persian Monarch and his Nobility; also the presents of those Jews who preferred to remain at Babylon.

Ezra then appointed Judges and Magistrates, and gave each of them their Commission, empowering them to enforce the Laws as laid down for the general government of the people.

Ezra maintained the supreme authority under his Commission from the Persian Court, during thirteen years, occupying himself with the faithful discharge of every part of his sacred duty, with unfeigned and pious zeal and assiduity. And still it seems that Ezra had not power or influence enough fully to accomplish by himself, his noble and praiseworthy enterprise.

About this time it was that Nehemiah, of whom we shall speak in the following Chapter, succeeded Ezra as Governor or Viceroy, and he brought with him a new Commission, with fresh power and authority from the Persian Court.

Ezra, now with a graceful and pious condescension, assumed a subordinate station. He acted as President to the Sanhedrin, the Grand Council of the Elders, and employed the whole of his time in reforming the Temple service, which had been sadly abused during the long captivity, and succeeded in restoring all its former rites and discipline. He carefully examined all the sacred Books, revised and corrected them. He then divided and fixed the number of Books to twenty-four, such as are now in use among the Hebrew Nation, called the Old Testament. Ezra was learned and well versed in them all; his high station and authority enabled him to collect the best copies from which to take the standard. In addition to all this, Ezra being himself inspired, and zealous in the sacred cause, and favored as he was with the valuable assistance of the three later Prophets, Haggai, Zachariah and Malachi, no doubt exists in the hearts of the Jewish Nation that the Bible now in their possession, is the same which existed in the days of the great Patriot for his God and his Religion, the inspired Ezra.

One of the strongest proofs that the Jews are correct in this respect is, that recent travelers have stated in all their journals, that wherever they met with Jews and their Synagogues they found a uniformity in the Scroll of the Law as read in the Jewish Church; besides, if we take into our consideration that Moses either wrote himself, or had written, thirteen copies of the Pentateuch, one of which he gave to each of the twelve Tribes, and the other he deposited in the Ark to remain there, in obedience to God's command in Deuteronomy, Chap, xxxi: 26, it is not at all surprising that the Jews have the original law in their possession, as handed down from Moses, the Divine Legislator.

When Nehemiah was established in his new Government, Ezra being relieved from the public duties and affairs of the State, now employed himself in expounding the Scriptures to the people, from morn till noon; and that he might be properly heard and understood, he had a platform fixed in one of the widest streets in the City. Ezra, himself, was raised upon the middle of the platform, and on each side of him stood the Priests, who were assistants and interpreters; and as Ezra read the Law in the Hebrew, the Priests explained it to the people in the Chaldee language, which had become familiar to them in consequence of their long sojourn in the great City of Babylon. In this way it was, that all the people of the Holy City, as well as those who came from very distant parts, especially on the Festivals and Holy days, could thus have the Bible and the Law explained to them, and their duty fully recommended to them every day, or at least regularly every Sabbath.

It must here be noticed, that all those Jews who had settled themselves in Alexandria and all the Grecian Provinces, had the Bible interpreted to them in the Greek language, after that the Bible had been translated into that language. From this circumstance it arose that those of the people who used the Greek language in the Synagogues, were called Hellenists, to distinguish them from those who continued the use of the Chaldee language.

The last work which Ezra performed, was, the restoring to the people the sacred service of the Temple, according to the original and usual form before the captivity. He revised and amended the Jewish Liturgy, adding many new prayers and forms of Thanksgiving composed since the return from Babylon, on the blessings of Liberty and freedom from bondage. This pious and truly religious man composed also the service used at the dedication of the new Temple; and he carefully arranged all the Psalms and Hymns chanted on that occasion by the Priests and the Levites, in the house of God. Many of the prayers above noticed, are still extant among the Jewish Nation, of which we shall have to speak in a future Chapter.

Ezra as a Priest, a Preacher of righteousness, and a skilful Scribe of the Law of God, unweariedly continued the reformation he had begun. He spent almost the whole of his time in preparing correct editions of the Holy Scripture—as during the captivity at Babylon, many copies had been lost, and many of them had been destroyed by the enemy—those which remained were chiefly in the hands of private individuals. Ezra, therefore, carefully examined these copies, and corrected those errors which may have been made, probably through the carelessness of the various transcribers.

It is stated, that in the Church of Saint Dominic, in Bononia, or Bologna, in Italy, there is a copy of the Law, kept with great care, said to be written by Ezra himself, upon leather made up into a roll according to the ancient manner, and in the same form as used now among the Israelites of the present day. This very eminent, pious and good man, may truly be said to be a second founder of the Jewish Church and State—a character highly esteemed, honored and beloved—zealous for his God, and anxious only for the happiness and welfare of his people.

Ezra had now been some years succeeded by his friend and coadjutor Nehemiah, whom Ezra had originally introduced at the Court of Persia; and to whom he had rendered every assistance in his power to enable him to discharge his mission with credit to himself, and satisfaction to the Government by whom he was engaged.

Ezra continued to employ the remainder of his life in the religious affairs of his Nation. There is some doubt entertained as to the place where he died—some suppose that he died and was buried in Jerusalem—others again assert that in his old age Ezra returned to the Court of Persia, and died there at the advanced age of one hundred and twenty years. Ezra brings down the history of his Nation to the twentieth year of Ahasuerus, the then reigning King of Persia.

CHAPTER III.

Of the affairs of the Jewish Nation during the days of Nehemiah.

This great and good man stands a noble example and instance of a zealous and disinterested patriot in the cause of religion and its Divine author.

Nehemiah was the son of Hechaliah, who was one of the captive Jews carried in early life to Shushan, the metropolis of Persia. He had been fortunate in obtaining an appointment in the Persian Court, and he chose rather to continue in his office at Court, than to return with his countrymen to Jerusalem.

Nehemiah was born at Shushan. He was a man of public spirit, learning and piety. He was appointed Cup-bearer to the King of Persia. In this office he obtained the royal favor, which made him much beloved at Court; and he thus became a man of great influence, and in the possession of considerable wealth. Nehemiah had never seen Jerusalem, although his ancestors had lived and died there; he, however, had at all times expressed himself kindly disposed towards his brethren, though strangers to him, and he anxiously wished for an opportunity to exercise the influence of his high position for their benefit.

Nehemiah was taking a walk one evening near Shushan, and seeing some travelers who appeared to be strangers going toward the city gates, curiosity led him to listen to their conversation, which was held in Hebrew. He saluted the strangers, and enquired of them from what country they came? Jerusalem, was the reply. Anxious to know something of his people, he entered deeply into conversation with the strangers, and earnestly sought all the information respecting his brethren in Jerusalem. He learned from the travelers that the walls of the City were broken down, and that the people were constantly being annoyed and plundered by the riotous banditti who infested the neighborhood; that there was no possibility of preventing these outrages, and that every morning the roads were strewed with the dying and the dead.

Nehemiah was so affected at the account of this deplorable situation of his brethren, that he burst forth into tears, and prayed fervently to God in their behalf. While thus engaged and agitated in mind, orders came from the Palace informing Nehemiah that the King demanded his presence. The King observing sorrow depicted in the countenance of his favorite Nehemiah, enquired the cause, in which enquiry, the Queen who was present, also joined, and seemed solicitous to know the reason of his apparent grief. The King kindly asked Nehemiah what was the cause for sorrow and tears? Nehemiah, encouraged by this favorable opportunity, explained to the King the cause of his grief, and related to him that which he had previously heard from the passing travelers. He then stated to the King that Jerusalem was the City of his ancestry; that the walls and gates were broken down by its enemies, and that all its inhabitants were being murdered by the robbers who infested the place. Nehemiah closed his sorrowful tale by presenting a petition to the King, praying that he might be commissioned to go to Jerusalem, and be empowered to repair the walls of the City.

The King in reply, said to Nehemiah, "Dry up your tears and be cheerful; your petition shall be granted, and an order shall be given to assist you in your noble and praiseworthy undertaking." The King then issued out immediate orders to Sanballat, and other officers of his Court, to furnish Nehemiah with money from the Royal Treasury, and every necessary material to carry out the proposed object. Nehemiah overflowing with joy and gratitude, fell down on his face and poured out his soul in thanks and praises to his Monarch for his inimitable goodness towards himself and his people. The King then granted to Nehemiah leave of absence from the Court, to fulfil the mission he had thus undertaken.

Nehemiah set out immediately for Babylon, and took with him a sufficient number of men to accompany him on his journey, together with a troop of guards which the King had given him as an escort. Thus equipped, Nehemiah and all his company arrived safely at the Holy City, Jerusalem. He here shut himself up three whole days in religious devotion and pious meditation. The three days being ended, Nehemiah went forth towards evening to examine the City and its walls. The report he had received from the travelers whom he saw at Shushan, proved to be quite true.

The next day Nehemiah assembled all the Elders and heads of the people, and made known to them his commission, and likewise his object in coming to Jerusalem. He then requested their co-operation, in order to fulfil the task he had imposed upon himself. The people readily assented to all which the good man proposed to them, and thus enabled him to complete the work in repairing and fortifying the walls. He engaged a numerous body of mechanics and their families, and diligently presided daily over the work himself, until the whole was completed.

The work being ended, and all in good order, Nehemiah with true piety and religious zeal, caused a Dedication to be solemnized by the Priests and the Levites, in gratitude to Almighty God, by whose mighty power and parental care alone, the people had thus far gained a victory over their unrelenting persecutors.

In the execution of this work, Nehemiah exhibited great courage, and exposed himself to many dangers and insults. He kept a body guard about him to protect him from the attacks of the enemy, and personally superintended the building of the walls. He made the laborers work in armour; both the mason and his man carried swords, with shields lying at their side, while trumpeters were placed at certain distances, to sound the alarm at the approach of the enemy. Nehemiah was once told of a conspiracy formed against him, by assassins who had determined to kill him, and his friends advised him to take refuge in the Temple, but Nehemiah nobly replied: "Should such a man as I flee? Who is there, being as I am, would go into the Temple to save his life? I will not go in!"

The walls of the City having been finished, which was the extent of the Commission granted to Nehemiah, he went back to Shushan to obtain further orders; and during his temporary absence, he entrusted the care of his Government and the City, to two of his brothers.

On the return of Nehemiah to Jerusalem, he set about fortifying the City, and beautifying the Temple. It was at this time that Ezra the Scribe delivered his public Lectures, as related in the history of that great man.

Nehemiah zealously and diligently corrected all the abuses and disorders in the State, as far as his influence and authority enabled him. He now called upon all the people for contributions to beautify and adorn the Temple, and for the support of its service; and in order to set a good example, he very liberally gave from his own purse a thousand drachms of gold, fifty dishes, and two hundred and fifty-two dresses for the Priests. He further arranged that the Priests and the Levites should be near the Temple, so that they should at all times be regular in their attendance at Divine Worship; for which purpose, Nehemiah had houses built in the immediate neighborhood of the Temple.

Nehemiah kept a princely table, a splendid equipage, and a train of servants, altogether at his own expense—exacting no tribute whatever from any one, but giving himself liberally, wherever it was required. Thus with the highest honor, credit and generosity, he completed the period of his Commission.

Nehemiah had now presided as Governor during twelve years; and therefore, according to his promise, he returned to the Court of Persia. After five years residence at Shushan, Nehemiah obtained permission to return to Jerusalem, and resume his office as Governor. On his return he found great depravity and corruption among the people, both in the

Church and the State. The people had sadly neglected the service in the Temple—they had profaned the Sabbath by making it a day of traffic, and following their usual avocations as on the other days of the week.

Nehemiah immediately assembled all the Magistrates and other officers of the State, and severely rebuked them for suffering the people to commit such outrages against their Holy Religion. He then ordered that the gates should be closed on every Friday, from sun set, until Saturday evening after dark—by which means all traffic was suspended—was, that the people were again brought into the practice of keeping the Sabbath Holy, and abstaining from all worldly matters during that sacred day.

Nehemiah strenuously persisted in his good work, by enforcing the observance of the Mosaic Law throughout the length and breadth of the land; he had Lectures delivered daily in Jerusalem, in the hearing of all the people, and the Pentateuch expounded in a language familiar to all the people. This practice was first carried out in the open streets, (as already noticed in the former Chapter,) or in the public market places, as found most convenient, until such time when arrangements could be made for the establishment of Schools and Synagogues suitable for such purposes. These Schools were, however, not built nor in full action until some time after the death of this venerable and pious man.

Nehemiah is supposed to be the last Governor of the Jews sent from the Court of Persia. The Government of Judea was afterwards conducted by the High Priests, till the days when Alexander the Great had totally ruined the Persian Empire. Nehemiah lived till he became very far advanced in years, happy in the love of his people, and in the success of his honest and disinterested labors. He recorded his own history, in which his name is transmitted to posterity with delight to all who read of his zeal, and his religious devotion to the welfare and improvement of his poor suffering brethren in Jerusalem.

This truly pious and zealous patriot had his recompense in this world, by the satisfaction he had, in seeing his good work carried out according to his ardent wishes and anxious desires. He, together with his cotemporary, the good Ezra, of whom we have already spoken, were devoted to the cause of true religion; they were not actuated by any worldly selfishness, or literary fame, for they only endeavored to restore the people to the original pure worship of the Temple, such as was commanded and practised by Moses and the Elders, and the subsequent generations, without any attempt on their part to introduce new laws for the government of the Synagogue or Temple worship; and hence they succeeded in their noble and pious undertaking. A bright example to all those whom God Almighty in his wisdom may be disposed to select as Priests or Chiefs over the people, to see that naught but the true spirit of religion be preached and practised among the people, to the honor and glory of Him who so graciously condescended to give his people a code of laws for their guidance and instruction, in every stage of existence. Nehemiah has transmitted a name and reputation to all generations, more honorable and durable than the Grecian Pillar, or the Roman Statue. His liberality, disinterestedness, courage and industry—his affectionate feelings and love for his country—will live in the hearts of his people forever and ever.

Before we close this Chapter, we must briefly notice some events of deep interest and importance to the Jews, which took place in Persia, during the days of Nehemiah. In the third year of the reign of Ahasuerus, King of Persia, the whole Nation of the Jews were in great danger of being destroyed through the wicked misrepresentations of a haughty and imperious Minister of the Persian Court; this was Haman, a descendant of Amalek, who was at all times a dire enemy of the Jewish race. The malicious designs of this crafty Amalekite, were frustrated by the inscrutable ways of an all-wise Providence, who never forsakes the good and the just, in the hour of distress. The King of Persia made a great Feast for his Captains and nobles, after which, he made another Feast for all the people who were found in the Metropolis of Shushan. On the seventh day of this banquet, the King commanded his Queen Vashti to appear in the grand chamber before all the company who were then assembled. It being contrary to the laws of Persia for ladies to be seen in public assemblies, the Queen refused to do the King's bidding. This refusal of the Queen greatly incensed the King; and having consulted his Council as to the mode necessary to be adopted on this occasion, the King at their advice, removed Vashti from the Court, and deprived her of all her regal glory. When the King began to reflect on his hasty decree, he became disconsolate, and sorely regretted the loss of his favored Vashti. His friends and counsellors seeing this change in the King's manners, divined the cause, and endeavored to divert him therefrom, by advising and recommending him to select for himself another Queen, in the place of Vashti. The King, on reflection, approved the advice, and accordingly issued a Commission, throughout all his dominions, to select the most celebrated beauties that could be found, and present them at court, from whom the King might select one as his future Queen.

Among the many ladies thus presented to the Persian Monarch, was a beautiful Jewess, named Esther, an orphan of both parents. She was brought up and educated under the kind care of her cousin Mordecai, a man of rank among the Jews, who was at that time living in the Capital of Persia.

The King, on seeing Esther, was so charmed with her personal appearance, the elegance of her deportment, and her exquisite beauty, that he immediately resolved to crown her as the future Queen of Persia; and accordingly in the seventh year of his reign, the nuptials were celebrated in great pomp and magnificence.

Esther now being at the Palace of the Persian Monarch, Mordecai considered it his duty to be near her, in order to watch over her as he did in the days of her youth—and for this purpose he took up his station in one of the King's gates. This enabled him to know all that was passing, without being particularly observed by those who frequented the Court. About this time a conspiracy was formed against the life of the King, by two of his attendants. Mordecai, having discovered the plot, made known the same to the King; an investigation took place, and the charge being fully sustained, the criminals were both executed, and the facts registered in the Persian records; but no other reward was given to Mordecai for his services.

The King's Prime Minister, Haman, had contracted a strong antipathy against Mordecai, who refused to pay homage to him in the manner he had exacted from all the King's household. Not content to punish Mordecai alone, for his supposed want of respect to Haman's dignity, he resolved to extirpate the whole race from off the face of the earth; and in order to accomplish this atrocious design, Haman represents to the king that the Jews were a people different from the rest of the king's subjects, and very disobedient to his laws. The king relying on the truth of the statement made by his favorite minister, and he offering to pay into the king's treasury 10,000 talents of silver to pay necessary expenses, the king gave him the power to do as he thought proper; and Haman accordingly appointed a day for the total extermination of the whole Jewish nation. This affair took place in the twelfth year of the king's reign, and about five years after Ezra had received his commission to go to Jerusalem.

Up to this period, none knew, not even the king himself, that queen Esther was a Jewess, for her cousin Mordecai had particularly enjoined her not to divulge her kindred, nor her nation. Strictly did Esther obey her cousin in everything that he conjured her; and the result was that her obedience to him, who was her second father and her natural guardian, proved to be the great contributing cause of her becoming the sole instrument in preventing her nation from being totally exterminated.

Mordecai having learned all that had passed in reference to this decree, sent a message to queen Esther informing her of all that had occurred, and imploring her to go to the king and petition him to save her people. The queen, on hearing this sad news felt sorely grieved, and was at a loss how to act, knowing as she did, that the laws of the Medes and Persians were unalterable; and that the ordinance had been passed, prohibiting any person, on pain of death, from approaching the king without being called to attend him, unless he should condescend to hold forth his golden sceptre as a signal of his pleasure. The queen sent a message to her cousin Mordecai, pointing out to him the danger of such an undertaking; to which he replied, that it was not her own personal safety that was in question, but the security of a whole race, who were unjustly condemned to perish by the vile artifices of an arrogant and ambitious man. Esther, feeling the force of the appeal made to her by Mordecai, repaired to the palace, at the risk of her own life, to save her people; and to her great joy and astonishment, the moment the king beheld her in the court, he kindly extended the sign of mercy, and gave her a favorable reception. Esther, encouraged by this pleasing invitation, related to her husband the intentions and plot of the wicked Haman, who was instantly condemned to death, and Mordecai was favorably admitted into the king's household as the relative of the queen. The king, by another royal edict, published throughout all his dominions, that the Jews should be empowered on the day named by Haman for their destruction, to stand on their own defense; and as this decree became known all over the land to be the real wishes of the sovereign, and Haman being no more, it proved serviceable to the poor Jews, and fully answered all that could have been expected; but yet, not without great slaughter among the people during the various conflicts and battles which took place on the day appointed. In these conflicts, the Jews standing only on their own defense, slew upwards of seventy-five thousand of their enemies, who rose up against them. It is in commemoration of this signal deliverance from their enemies, that the feast of Purim is celebrated annually among the Jews throughout the world.

Without referring to any particular cause, there is no doubt that the influence of Esther, and that of Mordecai, who became high in honor, and a favorite at the court of Persia, must have proved very beneficial to the Jews in general, and especially those who were in Jerusalem. Mordecai being now in power, promoted all his kindred to posts of honor, dignity and emolument; and through his influence, many of his countrymen became wealthy and prosperous. Here we may observe how the overruling providence of God is signally displayed. Mordecai retained his influence with the king, being the next in the administration; he was beloved and revered by all his brethren, whose happiness and welfare were his constant study.

It is stated, that in a place called Amdam, in Persia, the tombs of both Mordecai and Esther are still to be seen, and are highly prized by all the Jews living in Persia and the adjacent countries.

CHAPTER IV.

Of the state of the Jewish Nation under the Persian and the Grecian Monarchies.

After the death of Nehemiah, Judea became subjected to those whom the Kings of Persia made Governors of Syria. These governors placed the regulation of affairs under the control of the high priest, who had all the sacred authority, as well as civil power, vested in him, but still he was under the direction of the governor of Syria. This arrangement, however, was frequently interrupted by the different governors and princes, from time to time, who occasionally appointed other persons, not of the family of the priests, to officiate in such sacred office.

It is recorded in the book of Nehemiah, that when Johannan, the son of Jehoiada, had been in possession of the royal priesthood during many years, Bagoses, the governor of Syria, appointed Jeshua the younger brother of Johannan to depose him, and take the priesthood to himself. This caused considerable disturbance and dissatisfaction; a tumult arose in the inner court of the Temple, and Jeshua was slain there by his brother.

Bagoses, the governor of Syria, incensed at such opposition to his views, immediately entered the inner court of the Temple, in defiance of the remonstrance of the Jews, who explained to him that he was unclean, and therefore unfit to enter the holy edifice. In reply, Bagoses proudly remarked "that he was purer than the dead carcass of him whom they had slain there;" and as a punishment for this outrage, he imposed a heavy fine for every lamb that was offered throughout the year.

About this period the Jews were most miraculously saved from the threatened oppression and resentment of Alexander the Great, king of Macedonia, in Greece, who had marched toward the city of Jerusalem with a powerful army, determined to punish the people for refusing to assist him in the siege of Tyre.

At the time when Alexander declared war against the people of Tyre, they were so wholly occupied as merchants that they had entirely neglected all agricultural pursuits, and consequently had to be supplied with provisions by their immediate neighbors. Judea was at this time the place from which they were mostly furnished with all that they required. Alexander was necessarily compelled to seek provisions from the same source, and accordingly sent his orders to that effect. The Jews had previously declared their allegiance to Darius, and considered that they were bound in faith not to acknowledge any new power during his lifetime, and therefore refused to obey the command of the proud Macedonian. Alexander, being then in the zenith of his glory, having been so eminently successful in his late wars, considered that every nation was bound to submit to him, and that he durst not be contradicted. The refusal of the Jews in this respect, greatly incensed Alexander; he marched towards Jerusalem determined to punish the Jews, as he had the Syrians, for not obeying his commands. The Jews, fearing the consequences of the Emperor's power, which was certainly great at that time, felt severely the dilemma into which they were thus innocently involved; and as usual with the chosen people of God when in distress, they had no other course to adopt but to rely on the protection of Him who had at all times responded to their call, in the hour of trouble. For this purpose all Jerusalem were assembled together in prayer and supplication, and offering additional sacrifices in the Temple—imploring the mercy of God in their great distress. The high priest then gave instructions that the gates of the city should be thrown open, and that all the priests should be clad in their official robes, (he himself being attired in his pontifical habiliments,) and that all the elders and heads of the nation should go forth to meet the conqueror in grand procession. On the approach of Alexander to the city, and beholding this imposing scene, he was smitten with profound awe and religious veneration. He saluted the high priest and tenderly embraced him—entered the city in the most friendly manner, declaring himself the friend and protector of Israel. The Syrians and Ph[oe]nicians, who being the enemies of the Jews, were in expectation that the Emperor would wreak his vengeance on them and destroy them as he had those of Tyre, surprised and disappointed at this sudden change of the Emperor's conduct, naturally enquired into the cause; to which Alexander replied, that while at Macedonia he had a dream, in which he saw the figure of the same high priest, dressed in his sacerdotal robes, encouraging him to pursue his expedition against the Persians, and promising him success; which was fully realized beyond his most sanguine expectations. In the person of the present high priest, he saw the same figure which had appeared to him at Dio, and therefore he concluded that his success was mainly attributable to the will of God; and that, in the person of the high priest, he paid adoration to God in gratitude for the favor thus conferred upon him.

Alexander, thus pacified, enquired of the Jews what favor they had to ask of him, which was in his power to grant; to which they replied, the privilege of being governed by their own laws, and to have no obstruction in following the religion of their forefathers, which was more dear to them than all worldly distinctions. This request was accordingly granted; and further, as a mark of Alexander's favor, they were to be exempt from paying tribute or taxes during the seventh year, because in that year they neither sowed nor reaped their land.

Alexander then requested the high priest to have a golden image of his likeness placed between the porch and the altar, as a memorial of his visit. The high priest in reply to the Emperor, explained to him that according to the Jewish law, it was forbidden to have any image or likeness set up in the house of God, which was exclusively devoted to the worship of Him who is the sole ruler of the universe. But, said the high priest, we will make a greater memorial for you, which shall descend to ages yet to come; that all the male children which shall be born unto the priests during the coming year, shall be named after your imperial majesty, in honor of your illustrious condescension and clemency on this momentous occasion.

The king expressed himself highly pleased with this promise of the high priest, and in token of his approbation presented a considerable amount of gold for the use of the Temple service. Alexander then retired, well satisfied with all that had transpired; and on leaving the Temple, he declared in a very fervent tone, "Blessed be the Lord God of Israel, the God of this house."

Alexander, on leaving Palestine, marched into Egypt, over which he made an easy conquest, as the people having heard of his success, immediately surrendered; and thus he became master of that country. He built the city of Alexandria, and peopled it with different nations, among whom were many Israelites, who enjoyed the same privileges with the rest of his subjects.

In the following spring, Alexander became perfect master of the whole of the Persian Empire; he then made war with India and conquered it. Elated with success in all his enterprises, he indulged in all the excesses of life, and within five years from this time he died from the effects produced by such an extravagant mode of life. A short time after his death, the Empire was divided among four of Alexander's generals, and then the Jewish nation fell into the power of Ptolemy Soter, who became master of Egypt, Arabia, Cael Syria, and Palestine of Judea, these countries being his share of the division of the Empire of Alexander.

The kings of Egypt and Syria being constantly at war with each other, and desirous of enlarging their dominions, the Jews were at a loss whose cause to support, as they were called upon by all parties. This placed them in extreme difficulties, being in danger on both sides, and consequently badly treated by both parties in power.

CHAPTER V.

Of the affairs of the Jewish Nation under Ptolemy Soter, Ptolemy Philadelphus, and Ptolemy Philopater, Kings of Egypt.

Ptolemy Soter signified his intention to make Alexandria, in Egypt, his capital city. He persuaded many of the Israelites to settle there, with the promise that the same privileges granted them by Alexander, should be continued to them. This boon induced numbers of Jews to settle in Alexandria.

A remarkable story is told of one Mossolam, a Jew, who was one of those who followed Ptolemy at this time. This Mossolam was one of a Jewish troop of horse, who were advised by some soothsayer to stand still at the sight of a bird which appeared in the air, and that the people should follow the direction of this bird, either to go one way or the other, as that bird took its flight; to test the truth of which, this Mossolam shot the bird with his arrow, and the bird fell dead at his feet. He then declared aloud to the people, "How could that poor bird foretell our fortune, which knew nothing of its own?" His object was, in this expression, to expose the superstition of the heathens, so prevalent in those days.

Ptolemy Soter established a college of learned men, at Alexandria, in Egypt, and commenced a library there, which Ptolemy Philadelphus, his youngest son and successor, improved to one hundred thousand volumes. It is stated that this prince ordered the Pentateuch to be translated into the Greek language, that the Gentiles might be enabled to read it; this was accordingly done, and placed in the great library, as we shall read hereafter.

This college of learned men was encouraged, and the library increased under the several Ptolemys till it contained seven hundred thousand books. This circumstance made Alexandria the place of residence and resort for learned men during several ages. It happened, unfortunately for posterity, that one half of this famous library was burnt by Julius Cæsar in his Alexandrian war, and the balance was finally destroyed by the Saracens, in the year 642 of the Christian era.

Ptolemy gained the favor of the Jews, by paying a ransom of one hundred thousand of their countrymen, who had been taken captive and made slaves in Egypt. Having thus ingratiated himself into their good opinions, he proposed the translation of the Pentateuch above mentioned, in the following manner: he selected six Elders out of each tribe, making the number of seventy-two; these he invited to his court, and engaged them to perform the task, which was accordingly done and approved by him; and in token of his approbation, he very liberally rewarded them for their labors. This translation is known by the name of the Septuagint—so called from the circumstance of there having been seventy-two learned men employed for that purpose. The Septuagint is, however, by no means considered a correct translation, there being many incongruities contained therein; the rendering of many passages being at variance with the original Hebrew. The translation of the prophets, etc., into Greek, was made many years later, in the days of Antiochus Epiphanes; this completed the translation of the whole of the Old Testament.

When Ptolemy Philopater reigned over Egypt and Syria, he persisted in offering up sacrifices in gratitude to the God of Israel, for his success against Antiochus the Great, the successor of Seleucus, king of Syria. The Jews naturally opposed this measure, and were consequently persecuted because of their strict adherence to their religion.

The kings of Syria and Egypt, in order to annoy the Jews, would force themselves into the holy Temple, and burn sacrifices upon the altar. It is related of Ptolemy Philopater that he insisted on entering even the holy of holies. The priests and the levites, and all the people, assembled together in prayer and supplication to the Almighty, to assist them in preventing the sanctuary from being polluted by the heathen. It happened that, when the king was about to enter the holy Temple, he was smitten with such terror and confusion of mind, that he was removed from the holy place almost lifeless.

The king, on his recovery from this attack, which he believed was caused by the prayers of the people, was determined to be revenged on the whole Jewish nation; for which purpose, he went to Alexandria, and commanded that all the people should sacrifice to his idols. The people in general refused to do so, on which account he deprived them of all the privileges which had been granted to them by Alexander the Great. He then directed that every Jew should be marked with an ivy leaf, (the same being the badge of his idol Bacchus,) burned in their flesh with a hot iron; and further, that all those who resisted this infliction, should either be made slaves or put to death. Some few of the poor Jews reluctantly obeyed the king's mandate, in order to prevent the threatened punishment; but many thousands of them stood firm in the religion of their fathers, and suffered all the persecutions of the tyrant, rather than forsake the God who had wrought so many miracles in their behalf.

Ptolemy, vexed to find that the people would not sacrifice to his idols, and that they submitted to every degradation rather than forsake their God, resolved to be revenged, and threatened to destroy and annihilate the whole of the nation; and this he attempted to do, by issuing an order that all the Jews who lived *in* and *about* Egypt, should be brought to Alexandria in chains, and there to be devoured by his elephants. The Jews were brought to the place of execution, where the elephants were made drunk with wine and frankincense, and then let loose among the people; but instead of falling upon the Jews, they turned their rage upon the spectators who came to witness the scene, and destroyed great numbers of them, leaving the Jews unhurt.

The king on seeing his plans frustrated, began to reflect, and to be convinced that the God of Israel would protect his people from their enemies; and fearing that he would become the victim of the vengeance of a justly offended God, he immediately revoked his cruel decree, and restored to the people all their former privileges. Those, however, who had forsaken their God and abandoned their religion by sacrificing to his idols, were delivered into the hands of their enemies, and many of them were put to death.

How just are the dispensations of Providence! and how secure is man under the most perilous circumstances, while he puts his trust in his God and remains firm to the true worship of Him who is ever watchful of the safety of his faithful and trustworthy followers.

CHAPTER VI.

Of the Jewish affairs under Antiochus the Greek, Seleucus, and Antiochus Epiphanes, Kings of Syria.

After the death of Ptolemy Philopater, Ptolemy Epiphanes came to the throne. The Jews, having experienced severe persecutions at the hands of the Ptolemys, surrendered to the power of Antiochus the Great, King of Syria; and when he came to Jerusalem, the people went out to meet him in great procession, and very graciously welcomed him to their city.

Antiochus, flattered by this mark of their attention granted them the same privileges as he had done to their brethren who had settled themselves in Babylon and Mesopotamia. He had at all times expressed himself satisfied with the conduct of the people, having found them on all occasions true and loyal subjects.

Antiochus, wishing to show his confidence in the Jews, and with a view of encouraging them, sent many of them from Babylon to Lower Asia, to guard and protect his forts and garrisons, and allowed them good settlements; hence many of the Jewish nation peopled that part of the country. At the death of Antiochus, his son, Seleucus Philopater, succeeded him. In his day, Simon, a Benjamite, was made Governor of the Temple. He had some difference with Onias, the high priest, who was a very good man. Simon, however, not succeeding in his expectations with the high priest, reported to Appolonius, the Governor of the Province under Seleucus, that great treasures were deposited in the Temple; upon which information Heliodorus, the treasurer, was sent to seize them.

Heliodorus accordingly repaired to the Temple to make this seizure. When he entered the Temple he found the priests and all the people engaged in solemn prayer to Almighty God, imploring his divine assistance in their present distress. The scene which thus presented itself to him at that moment so powerfully affected him, that he fell prostrate before the Lord of Hosts, whose power he publicly acknowledged, and resolved not to interfere with the people of God, as he called them, and immediately left the city.

Antiochus Epiphanes succeeded his brother Seleucus in the kingdom of Syria. When seated on the throne, Jason, the brother of Onias the high priest, bribed Antiochus with a large sum of money to deprive Onias of the priesthood and to banish him to Antioch; at the same time Jason wished to have the priesthood conferred on him; not, as it is supposed, that he wished to have it as a religious office, but because it would invest him likewise with the power of the civil government. Antiochus received the bribe; banished Onias to Antioch, and then appointed Jason to the office of high priest.

When Jason became high priest, he erected a place of exercise at Jerusalem for training up youth according to the fashion of the Greeks, and induced many of them to forsake the religious customs and usages of their forefathers, and to conform in many things to the customs and ceremonies of the heathens. Some few years after Jason had been in office, he commissioned his brother Menelaus to go to the court of Syria to pay the annual tribute money. Menelaus took advantage of this opportunity, and offered the king a larger bribe than his brother had given for the priesthood.

Antiochus made no scruple in the matter, and accepted the money thus offered by Menelaus; and gave instructions to his secretary to make out a fresh commission in favor of Menelaus, who returned triumphantly to Jerusalem, deposed his brother Jason, and placed himself in the office of the priesthood.

Menelaus being in office, abused the power and authority vested in him, and conducted himself in a manner much worse than his brother whom he had deposed. He stole some of the golden vessels from the Temple, impoverished the country, and by degrees he managed to enslave the whole of Judea, and overturned all that was left of her religion and her freedom. He then visited Antioch, where he met his brother Onias, who rebuked him for his misconduct both towards him and the people in general. Menelaus, chagrined at his brother's rebuke, adopted means by which Onias was put to death. During this time, Lysimachus, who had been appointed by Menelaus to officiate as his deputy during his absence, stripped the temple of many of its most costly vessels. He also committed many other sacrilegious acts; this occasioned a great tumult and confusion among the people, which ended in considerable bloodshed, and in which conflict the deputy himself fell a victim.

This circumstance led to a false report being industriously circulated, that Antiochus had fallen in the affray. Jason, availing himself of this confusion, headed an army of resolute and desperate men; repaired to Jerusalem which he assaulted; succeeded in putting to flight his brother Menelaus with his party, and committed great havoc among those who opposed him. Jason, however, was in the end defeated; his party routed; he himself perished in some strange land, and it is supposed even without the usual rites of burial.

Antiochus hearing of this affair, and imagining that Judea had revolted, gave immediate orders to his soldiers to repair to Jerusalem and to kill young and old without any reserve. The soldiers obeyed their cruel master in so unmerciful a manner, that in less than three days upwards of forty thousand souls were slain; thousands taken into captivity, and sold as slaves to the several neighboring nations.

Antiochus then entered the holy Temple, stripped it of all the sacred vessels still remaining—the altar of incense—the golden table and the golden candle-stick.

He then destroyed all the beautiful decorations of the House of God, robbed the noble edifice of all its treasures, and impiously polluted the holy of holies. And to further satiate his cruel revenge, he sacrificed a sow on the altar of burnt offerings, and scattered its fragments over every part of the Temple. The tyrant then departed, leaving the city of Jerusalem overwhelmed in sorrow and in mourning. The streets were strewed with the dying and the dead. The cries and lamentations of the orphan and the widow deplored the loss of their natural protectors and their property, which the tyrant carried away with him to enrich his unholy possessions.

Some time after, Antiochus sent his general Appollonius to collect the annual tribute to which the Jews were subject, and at the same time commanded him at the head of a thousand men, to attack the city of Jerusalem on the sabbath day, while the people were all engaged in their religious worship in the Temple.

Appollonius fully executed the mandate of his cruel master. He slew the priests and the Levites while at their sacred duties, together with numbers of the private citizens; led the women and children into captivity; destroyed all their houses; built a castle near the Temple, and placed a troop of men as guards to watch and annoy those few Jews who still remained in the city.

Not yet satisfied, the cruel tyrant issued a decree throughout all his dominions to suppress every religion excepting the worship of the idols, he himself had set up, and to which alone he paid his adoration. He forbade the Jews to perform the initiatory rite on their male children, and prevented them from offering any more sacrifices in the Temple to the God of Israel. He then set up an image upon the altar, and sacrificed to it, and called it the Temple of Jupiter Olympus. He compelled the people to offer up the flesh of swine, and other unclean beasts, and even to eat of them. He forced the Jews to profane the sabbath, and cruelly persecuted all such who did not strictly conform to his wishes; rendering the position of the poor Jews pitiable in the extreme, and probably unequalled by any other nation in the annals of the world. Antiochus then ordered all the books of the law, and other books used for worship, to be destroyed; and to effectually carry out his cruel edict, officers were appointed to search every house, and every person was examined on oath as to the possession of any Hebrew books or tablets. By this means not a copy of the law was to be seen among the poor Jews. Notwithstanding all these persecutions, there were found numbers of the people who defied the power of the merciless king; and putting their trust in the God of Israel, would not defile themselves with the idolatrous worship then imposed on them, and break the law of God. Sad to relate, that daily and hourly these people who adhered to their religion, were put to the sword and other torments, to compel them to act in obedience to the king's orders. Their love for their religion was greater than the pleasures of this world, and in support of that religion they sacrificed their own lives and those of their wives and children.

In the next and following chapters we shall inform our readers of the manner in which the Lord raised up champions in Israel, who valiantly and bravely resented the injuries inflicted on their countrymen, and zealously fought the battles of the Lord; the success which ensued, together with the total defeat of their enemies, and the punishment which awaited the tyrant Antiochus and his army.

CHAPTER VII.

Of the state of the Jewish Nation in the days of Mattathias the Priest, the father of the valiant Maccabees.

In the days of the tyrant Antiochus, who so frightfully and cruelly persecuted the Jews, there lived at Modin a very learned, pious, and noble priest; he was of the family of the Asmoneans, named Mattathias. This zealous and brave man was one of the first who was determined to oppose the future progress of Antiochus. Mattathias, who was known to be a man of considerable influence among his brethren, was highly complimented by the king's officers, and tempted by them to comply with the request of the king to renounce the Jewish religion and embrace that of the heathen. The priest boldly and fearlessly rejected their entreaties; and in the hearing of all the people he declared that no consideration whatever should induce him, or any of his family, to forsake his God and his holy religion; they would continue to walk in the sacred path of their fathers, and that no king on earth could be found to compel them to adopt any heathen worship.

This bold declaration of the valiant priest, created great sensation among the people—and some of them fearing the torments threatened to be inflicted on all such who refused to obey the king's orders, consented to offer sacrifices on the altar set up for heathen worship; this altar was placed at Modin. The priest, zealous in the cause of his religion, was determined to be avenged of this outrage committed by some of his brethren; he exhorted the people in general, not to be led away by the acts of these apostates, but to remain true to their holy faith, and that he and his family would pour out their life's blood for their sacred cause.

At this time a Jew presented himself at the altar, and sacrificed to the idol there erected. Mattathias, fired by religious zeal, fell upon the apostate and slew him on the spot. His sons, actuated by the same religious spirit, slew the king's chief officer and his men who enforced his wicked commands. They then destroyed both the altar and the images, declaring aloud to all their brethren, "Ye who are zealous for the cause of the Lord and His religion, follow us! Follow, follow!" The priest then collected together all the members of his family, and took up his abode in the neighboring mountains. Many of the Jews followed this example, and fled—some to the deserts, some to the mountains, and there assembling together, formed themselves into a little army—bold, resolute, zealous and brave in their just and noble cause.

The king's troops pursued them, and attacked them on the Sabbath day. The people unwilling to profane the Sabbath, made no resistance, unanimously declaring, "Let us rather die in innocence than triumph in guilt." The enemy taking advantage of this, slew them in great numbers. The venerable Mattathias grieved at seeing his brethren so cruelly and innocently murdered, made a decree, (having previously consulted his brother priests,) and published it throughout the land, that it should be lawful, should it be found requisite, for the people to defend themselves against their enemies, in the event of their being attacked, on the Sabbath day. This resolution was adopted and followed in all the subsequent wars, under the direction of their able and pious champions.

When Antiochus heard of this bold and daring resolution, so much beyond his expectations, he perpetrated the most frightful cruelties on every Jew who would not forsake his religion. On this occasion happened the martyrdom of the venerable and pious Eleazer, a priest of great learning, probity and zeal in the cause of religion. At the advanced age of ninety years, this poor man was led forth to the scaffold, and was desired to make a public declaration that he would renounce his religion—that he should eat swine's flesh in the presence of all the people, as a proof of his conversion. With resolute firmness, and becoming resentment, the venerable priest refused to comply with the wishes of the tyrant, and preferred death rather than forsake the religion of the one true God.

At this period it occurred, that a mother and her seven sons were scourged in order to compel them to eat swine's flesh. Both the mother and her sons publicly declared their resolution to die under the hands of the executioner, rather than transgress the laws of God. The tyrant then ordered their limbs to be cut off, their tongues to be cut out, and the skin of their heads to be stripped off with the hair; all which was executed in the presence of the mother, who encouraged her children to suffer their tortures bravely in the cause of their religion. She soothed their afflictions by the tenderest affections, beseeching them to fear God, and not the tyrant—and patiently to endure the torment, in the hope and expectation of a happy and glorious resurrection, where she would meet them again in mercy, and under the protection of an all gracious father, who never forsakes the truly righteous. The mother having witnessed the sufferings of all her sons, martyrs to the cause of their religion, shared the same sad fate, and under similar torments was ushered into eternity.

What a noble example to parents of the present day to watch over the conduct of their children, and exert all the means in their power to induce them to walk in the path of virtue; to inculcate in them true religion, and not suffer them to think so lightly of the precepts of the Lord—for it must be admitted that the apathy evinced in the present day by all classes of society, is the sole contributing cause of the infidelity so prevalent amongst us. If we are asked what is the cause of this infidelity, the answer is, the Holy Bible is not studied sufficiently, either privately or publicly; and not being understood, is consequently rejected by thousands of those who grow up in ignorance; hence, in the hour of distress, they have nothing to console them, as in olden times, as exhibited in the history before us.

During this time, Mattathias who still remained concealed in the mountains, encouraged his brethren to remain firm in their cause. He spoke so emphatically to them that he gained their confidence, in consequence of which, great numbers declared themselves true to the noble enterprise before them. Those who more particularly were devoted to the cause, were such as were called *chasideem*, or pious; of this sect we shall have to speak in a future chapter, and therefore we shall proceed with our narrative, in which we shall see the result of true piety and honest zeal in the defence of upright principles.

Mattathias and his party then marched, well armed, through all the towns and villages, destroyed all the altars and places of worship belonging to the heathens. They then circumcised all the male children, who had been neglected in this matter in consequence of the edict passed by the tyrant Antiochus. In this affair they met with very strong opposition, and in their defence they committed great slaughter among their enemies. They succeeded on this occasion in recovering many copies of the law, which had been hid at the time the mandate was issued to destroy all the copies of the law, or any other Hebrew manuscripts which might be found among the people. The venerable and pious priest had now grown grey in the service, and appeared to be fast approaching the verge of the grave. Sensible of his position, Mattathias assembled together all his children, together with his friends, and on his death bed he thus addressed them:

"My sons, be ye valiant and zealous in the cause I have so long advocated—expose your lives in its defence, and hereafter you will share the glorious reward of your perseverance. Let me, says the dying man, bring to your memory the spirit, the noble spirit and pious zeal of your ancestors, to animate your hope, and to encourage your steady reliance on the power and protection of your all-gracious God. Thus inspired, my dear children, and thus determined to defend your laws, your liberties, and your religion, you *will* not, you *cannot* fail of success. My son Simon has proved himself a man of wisdom, follow his advice as a father, and as a counselor. Judas, your brother, is well known for his courage and valorous conduct, let him be your general, let him head your army and lead you to the battle-field. My sons, may God Almighty ever protect you and prosper you in all your righteous undertakings, and crown all your laudable efforts with success."

After this tender and affectionate interview, this, his last and farewell advice to his sons, Mattathias in a good old age expired, and was honorably buried at Modin, in the sepulchre of his ancestors—beloved and esteemed by all who knew him in life, and revered and lamented by all who attended his mortal remains to the grave.

CHAPTER VIII.

The Government of the Jewish nation under the Maccabees, or as they were otherwise called, the Asmoneans, this being the family name.

Judas, at the dying request of his father, and with the full consent of his brothers, took upon himself the command of the forces, and at once erected his standard. Judas is henceforth called Judas Maccabees, because he chose for the motto of his banner in the field of battle, the sentence from the song of Moses, Exodus, chap, XV: "Who is like unto thee, amongst the powers, oh Lord!" In Hebrew the initials of the words in the sentence form the word "*Mochbee*." Hence it is, that all those who fought under the banner of Judas, were called "*Maccabees*," and all of that race were known by that name.

Judas and his brethren achieved many very valiant deeds, in defending the cause of the holy law, and the holy religion of the God of Israel, of which they were the bold champions. Judas was successful in gaining the many battles he fought with Antiochus; and to encourage his army to fight bravely, he exhorted them to put their trust in God and that they would conquer. This inducement held out to the army, appears to have produced the desired effect.

The tyrant Antiochus, seeing their repeated success, became resolute and determined to be avenged of his powerful opponents, the Maccabees. To effectuate this, he adopted the following stratagem: when he went into Persia to gather the tribute of the countries round about, he left Lysias with half his army, with express orders to destroy and root out all the Jews from their land.

Lysias proved as cruel as his master; he collected numerous forces and encamped near Jerusalem; his army consisted of forty thousand foot, and seven thousand horse. Encouraged by the hope of success on the part of Lysias, a body of merchants, about a thousand in number, repaired to the place of action, provided with large quantities of gold and silver, with the full expectation of buying the captive Jews for slaves. Whilst the enemy contemplated a complete victory, Judas and his brethren gathered themselves together unto Mizpah; here they fasted, put on sackcloth, and prayed to God to help them in their great distress. They opened the book of the law before God, where the heathens had polluted it by painting their images which they worshiped. They then sounded the trumpets and prepared for battle, resolved to a man to die in defence of their country and their religion. The result of this zeal and courage on the part of Judas, proved successful; Judas and his army put to flight and destroyed several large forces which Lysias had sent against them. They drove the enemy out of Jerusalem, and almost out of the land of Judea, and succeeded in possessing themselves of a large booty, both from the army and the merchants, who expected to become their masters.

Judas and his party, grateful to heaven for this great and glorious success over such powerful enemies, immediately repaired to Mount Sion, where they saw the sanctuary of God made desolate, deserted and neglected; even the altar was polluted, the gates and walls thrown down, the courts of the Temple, the beautiful edifice itself bedecked, not with sweet or odoriferous herbs, but with wild shrubs and grass which the hand of time had allowed to grow on that sacred spot. What a heart-rending scene for the pious Judas and his followers! Grieved at beholding such a devastation of God's holy place, they fell on their faces, rent their clothes, and made great lamentations; at the same time imploring the aid of heaven to repair the loss thus sustained.

Judas and his party diligently applied themselves to repair the Temple, and to restore the worship of God. They selected some of the good priests to purify the sanctuary; they removed the altar, which had been profaned by the heathens, and built a new one as the law directs. They then made some new vessels for the use of the Temple, from the gold which they had taken from the enemy in the late battle. The regular order of divine worship was again introduced, and sacrifices offered up according to the law of Moses.

It is somewhat remarkable, and worthy of our attention, that that very day three years, on which the heathen had profaned the altar by offering up unclean beasts, the Temple was dedicated with great rejoicings and grateful acknowledgments to God, which continued during eight days. It was on this occasion that Judas and his brethren ordained that this feast of dedication should be celebrated annually on the return of this period, with mirth and gladness, together with praises and thanksgiving to God. This feast of dedication is known among Israelites by the name "*Honucha*," Hebrew word for dedication. The fact related is, that when Judas and his men had purified the Temple, a very small lamp of consecrated oil was miraculously found, capable of furnishing sufficient to supply all the established holy lights in the Temple during eight days, until a fresh portion could be procured. This circumstance occurred about two years after Judas had the chief command, and upwards of three years after the city and the Temple had been laid desolate by Appollonius. History informs us, that the holy worship in the Temple continued with little interruption from the heathen, until the destruction of the Temple by the Romans, though Jerusalem itself was often in the power of its enemies.

Notwithstanding the success achieved by Judas and his party, they were much annoyed by their enemies, from the fact that the fortress built by Appolonius still remained in the hands of the heathens. It stood on Mount Acra, a rising ground facing the Temple. The heathens placed themselves here to annoy the Jews, on their going to, and returning from the Temple. Judas finding that he could not drive out the enemy at once, endeavored to prevent these annoyances by building up Mount Sion with high walls and strong towers. He also placed guards there to protect the priests and the people when they went to the Temple, with the view of preventing the Gentiles from invading the sanctuary.

Though Judas and his men continued the Temple worship, they were still in constant warfare. The neighboring nations were all jealous of the success gained by the Jews, and dissatisfied that they had restored the sacred worship in the Temple of the Lord. To show their displeasure they attacked the Jews on all sides; war ensued, and fierce battles were fought, in most of which Judas proved victorious, sustaining but little loss in his army.

Judas, encouraged by such success, which he always acknowledged to be from the hand of God, and not from his own power, led forth his army against Georgius, a general of Antiochus, as also against the Idumeans, who had in their turn proved vexatious to the Jews. In these attacks Judas lost many of his men, but nevertheless proved victorious. Judas was a noble and valiant general; his policy was at all times to encourage his men by inducing them to put their trust in God, who had done so much for their ancestors, and instilling in their minds the belief that he would continue his protection to them as long as they were inclined to act righteously to each other. During this time, Antiochus was visiting Persia in order to receive his tribute from the people of that country—and plunder the Temple of *Diana*, erected at *Elymos*, which was said to contain great riches in gold and silver, and a very valuable armory. The people of Persia having gained intelligence of the king's intention, boldly defended the Temple of their idol, and succeeded in totally defeating the enemy.

Antiochus enraged at this discomfiture, and at the reports he had received of the defeat of his generals in Judea, resolved to march toward Jerusalem, and threatened to make the whole city as one grave, in which to bury all the Jews then in the Holy Land. How far this wicked man succeeded in his cruel resolve, the following facts will show; they need no comment on our part, to prove that it was the finger of God that was directing all that befel Antiochus, and other persecutors of mankind. It is generally supposed by historians, that the same disaster which befel the tyrant Antiochus, was visited on many persecutors of God's people, both in former and latter times—hence supporting our views on the subject, that Heaven ordained all that had happened. Whilst on his journey, Antiochus was smitten with an incurable plague; his chariot was upset, and he was seriously hurt. He was then carried to a small town on the road side, put to bed, in which he lingered for some time, suffering the most excruciating agonies of body, and torments of mind, until he died. On his death-bed, Antiochus showed great contrition of mind for the crimes which he had perpetrated against God and man. The heathens declared that it was a punishment inflicted for his intended sacrilege of the Temple of Diana; but the Jewish historians acquaint us, that the tyrant himself imputed his sufferings as a punishment for the cruelties towards Israel, and the impieties he practised against the Lord and his holy Temple. Thus ended the life of this great and relentless tyrant.

The pleasing tidings of the death of the tyrant having reached the ears of Judas, he was encouraged to besiege the garrison of the Syrians, in the town of Acra, in which enterprise he succeeded by a stratagem which will be hereafter related.

At the death of Antiochus Epiphanes, his son Antiochus Eupator became his successor. He proved to be no better than his father, whose footsteps he followed by persecuting the Jews wherever found throughout his empire. Antiochus Eupator commenced his career by bringing a vast army against Judas, consisting of one hundred thousand foot, twenty thousand horse, thirty-two elephants, and three hundred armed chariots of war. Judas's army being so small, compared with that of the enemy, encouraged his men by the watchword which he issued among them: "Victory is of the Lord." Animated by the hope of success, they managed to surprise the enemy at night, and slew upwards of four thousand of them, and then made a safe retreat to Jerusalem. In this encounter, Eleazer, one of the brothers of Judas, evinced great courage; he saw one of the elephants raised much higher than the rest. Supposing that the king himself must be mounted thereon, he ran through the camp, made his way to the beast, and thrust him through with his spear. The wound proving mortal, the beast with his heavy burthen fell down and crushed Eleazer to death.

Antiochus Eupator's army then marched to Jerusalem under the command of Lysias, and besieged the sanctuary. During this siege, the Jews suffered much from the want of provisions. They were on the point of surrendering to the enemy, when, by the providence of the Almighty, they were strangely released from the impending danger. It happened that Lysias, the general, heard that the city of Antioch was seized by one Philip, a favorite of the late king, who had taken upon himself the government of

Syria; Lysias, on this account, persuaded the present king to declare peace with the Jews, to which proposal he readily consented.

About this time Demetrius, the cousin of Antiochus, became king in his place, under the following circumstances: Demetrius was the son of Seleucus Philopater, the eldest brother of Antiochus Epiphanes; at his death, Seleucus endeavored to persuade the Romans to assist him in obtaining the kingdom of Syria, but without success. Being disappointed in his expectations, Demetrius went to Syria and there induced the people to believe that the Romans had sent him. On the strength of this report, Antiochus Eupator, and his general, Lysias, were seized by their own soldiers, and put to death by order of Demetrius.

Demetrius being seated on the throne, one Alcimus, a descendant of the tribe of Aaron, applied to him to be assisted in procuring the appointment of high priest, to which office he had been raised by the late king, Antiochus Eupator. Alcimus had been refused by the Jews, he having complied with the heathen superstition in the time of the persecution, in order to gain favor with the king and his generals. Judas and his party, now, as before, strenuously opposed the appointment of Alcimus, though strongly recommended by Demetrius. This opposition to his wishes, induced Demetrius to send one Bacchides to enforce the command of the king, but to no purpose. Demetrius then selected Nicanor, who was master of his elephants, as the future governor of Judea, with instructions to kill Judas, and bring the people under still greater subjection. Nicanor was at first unwilling to make war against Judas, but being urged on by the king, he pursued it with fresh fury; he boldly declared his intention to demolish the Temple at Jerusalem, and build one on the same spot in honor of the idol Bacchus. Nicanor was slain in the battle, and his army entirely routed by Judas and his party. Judas, desirous of making an example of this wicked man, for his blasphemous words which he uttered against the Temple of the Lord, cut off the head and right hand of Nicanor, and placed them in a conspicuous situation on one of the towers in Jerusalem. Judas then gave orders that a day should be annually appointed as a day of thanksgiving, in memory of this victory, which was called Nicanor's day. This day is not however celebrated as a holiday among the Jews in the present generation; it has been discontinued for many ages past.

At this period the Romans were growing great and powerful; Judas, aware of the danger likely to result from such power, deemed it advisable for the good of his country to propose a league with the Romans, to which they readily consented, and acknowledged the Jews as their friends and allies. Demetrius then received orders not to interfere with the Jews any more. Unhappily for Judas and his people, before the orders had reached Demetrius, he had already despatched Bacchides a second time to avenge the course of Nicanor, who had been slain, and to insist on establishing Alcimus in the priesthood. This circumstance proved very unfortunate for both Judas and his countrymen. Judas having but three thousand men with him, was overpowered by the strong forces of Bacchides; so little chance was there of success on the part of Judas, that many of his men deserted him through fear and fright. Judas, brave and valiant to the last in defence of his country's cause, and scorning to flee even for his life, fell a victim to the fury of the enemy.

The death of Judas created great excitement among the people, and sorely depressed their spirits. They became absorbed in sorrow and in grief for the loss of their noble chieftain. The people had fallen into such a state of lethargy, that they became an easy prey to the tyrant Bacchides, who, taking advantage of this state of things, committed great havoc among the people, and put to the sword all of Judas's friends and companions on whom he could lay hand.

Alcimus also availed himself of this opportunity, and exercised his authority in the office of the priesthood. He introduced into the worship of the Temple, imitations of heathen idolatry, and gave orders that the sanctuary should be thrown open, with equal freedom and liberty, both to Gentiles and to Jews. Alcimus, however, did not long prosper in his wicked career; in a very short time he was struck with palsy, deprived of his speech, and ultimately died in great anguish of mind and torment of body.

After the death of Judas Maccabees, his brother Jonathan was unanimously appointed by the people as their leader. Jonathan was ably assisted by his brother Simon; they both bravely resisted the many inroads made upon them by their enemies. Bacchides finding himself so powerfully opposed, sued for peace, which was granted on condition that he should restore all the captive Jews, depart from Judea forever, and in no way molest the people of that country. These conditions were cheerfully accepted by Bacchides, who left Judea in peace and in tranquility.

Jonathan, happy in having restored peace, commenced to govern his people under the old Jewish polity; he resumed all the rites and ceremonies of the Jewish religion, and succeeded in obtaining the confidence of his people by the zeal which he evinced in the performance of the duties of his office.

After the death of Alcimus, the office of high priest remained vacant seven years, when a man calling himself Alexander, appeared, and declared that he was a son of Antiochus Epiphanes. He seized the kingdom of Africa, and solicited Jonathan to join him against Demetrius, who had proved himself a formidable enemy of the Jews. As an inducement to Jonathan, Alexander made the following proposals to him: That Jonathan should be constituted both the Governor and the High Priest of the Jews, and be called the king's friend and counselor.

Jonathan considering these proposals likely to prove beneficial to his people, and there not being any one else for the priesthood, consulted them on the subject, and with their unanimous consent he accepted the offer made by Alexander.

At the following Feast of Tabernacles, Jonathan was duly installed in his new office, and vested with the sacerdotal robes usually worn by the high priests. Being thus dignified, he joined Alexander, and proceeded to battle against Demetrius, whose army was totally routed, and he himself, slain on the battle field.

It is said that from this time forward the high priesthood continued in the family of the Asmoneans or Maccabees, till the days of Herod, who changed it from an office of inheritance to an arbitrary appointment. Herod appointed those whom he pleased, without reference to merit or ability. This practice was continued until the total extinction of the priesthood at the final destruction of the Temple by the Romans.

Jonathan succeeded by his judicious conduct, in securing for his people their possessions, with free scope to exercise all their religious rites, without any interruption from their neighbors. He occasionally extended his assistance to those of the nations who proved kind to him, by which means the bond of friendship became strongly cemented between both parties.

Like most great men, Jonathan had his enemies: among them was one Tryphon, who sought to possess the kingdom of Syria, and by whose treachery, Jonathan was made prisoner in Ptolemais, and was afterwards cruelly murdered, together with his two sons.

The death of Jonathan and his two sons caused great lamentations among the people. Being in constant fear of their enemies, and now without a leader, they were at a loss what to do. In this dilemma they applied to Simon, the only surviving brother of Judas, to become their chief. Simon consenting to become their general, a council of war was called, at which meeting he was unanimously appointed and vested with power equal to his predecessors. Simon having been regularly installed into his new office, commenced his career by addressing his brethren in the following manner:

"You, my countrymen, are not ignorant how bravely my father, brothers, and myself, have fought in defence of our laws and our religion, our Temple and our people. They have sacrificed their lives in that glorious cause; I, only I, survive to maintain it. God forbid I should value my life at a higher price than they did theirs. Behold me then as they were, to glory in this undertaking, to die in defence of our nation, our Temple, our wives and our children." "Take courage my friends; the Lord is with us, and success will crown our righteous intentions."

Simon at the request of the people, then assumed the sacred office of the priesthood.

Having now entered into his new office, he procured the dead bodies of his brother Jonathan and his two sons, and buried them with great honors in the sepulchre of his fathers at Modin, and erected a stately monument to their memory.

Simon then repaired the fortresses and the walls of the city, which had been destroyed by their enemies, built for himself a very splendid mansion, and made Jerusalem his place of residence, where he held his court. The Jews were still annoyed by the garrison on the tower of Acra, when they went to and returned from the Temple. Simon succeeded in shutting up the enemy so closely in the tower that many perished from famine, which made the survivors surrender the tower. Simon being in possession of the tower, he, with the sanction of the people, pulled it down, and lowered the mount in such a way so that it could no more be made available for the purpose of annoying the people when assembled at their worship in the Temple.

Simon now turned his attention to the repairs of the sanctuary. He enforced a rigid observance of the laws of God, and successfully introduced peace and unanimity of feeling among the people. The nation at large, sensible of the good conduct of their leader, convened a general meeting of all the elders, priests and magistrates at Jerusalem.

At this meeting it was unanimously resolved, that the office of Governor of the nation, and that of the high-priesthood, should be henceforth vested permanently in Simon and his posterity after him, so that the said office should be hereditary in his family for ever. It was further decreed that an account of the noble deeds of Simon and his family should be engraven on a tablet, and placed in the Temple as an everlasting memorial, and that a copy of the same should be placed on the records in Judea. This excellent priest was held in such high estimation by all the surrounding nations, that the Romans sought his friendship, entered into a covenant with him, and conferred on him many honors.

The king of Syria followed the example of the Romans, and entered into a similar covenant with Simon.

The king of Syria, however, was not true to his covenant, he having after a time invaded Judea. Simon assisted by his two eldest sons, bravely defended themselves, and drove the enemy away with great discomfiture.

Simon continued to maintain a high reputation in his office for about eight years. He was at all times employed in providing for the comfort and welfare of his people. Simon now set out to examine into the affairs of his country, accompanied by his two sons, Judas and Mattathias. Having arrived at Jericho, they were invited by Ptolemeus, the son-in-law of Simon, to a banquet which he had prepared for them. Simon readily accepted this polite invitation of his relative, not suspecting in the least any treachery on the part of Ptolemeus, who had already concerted his plans with the court of Syria to destroy his father-in-law and his two sons who were then with him. While the guests were indulging at the banquet, Simon and his two sons were inhumanly murdered by order of Ptolemeus. He then dispatched a party to the residence of John, another son of Simon, who was captain of the forces at Judea, with orders to murder him also. John fortunately gained intelligence of all that had occurred at Jericho to his father and brothers, as also the plot laid for him. He courageously and bravely defended himself, and cut to pieces the enemy.

John then fled to Jerusalem for safety. Ptolemeus followed him, and arriving at the same time, they both presented themselves at different gates. From the respect the people had for Simon and his ancestors, John was received by the people with open arms, whilst the murderer of Simon and his two sons, was repulsed with all his followers. John was then unanimously appointed to succeed his father, both in the government and the priesthood. He was then surnamed Hyrcanus, and henceforward known by the name of John Hyrcanus.

CHAPTER IX.

Of the Jewish affairs under the conduct of the posterity and successors of Simon the Maccabee.

Antiochus Sidetes, being informed of the death of Simon, and being invited by Ptolemeus, invaded Judea again, besieged Jerusalem, and reduced Hyrcanus and the Jews to the last extremity of famine. Hyrcanus then sued for peace, which was granted on the condition of paying certain tributes to the king, and removing the fortifications of Jerusalem. A few years after, Antiochus died, which occasioned great confusion among the surrounding nations; Hyrcanus took advantage of this to enlarge his territories, by seizing some neighboring towns round about Judea, and renounced all further dependence on the kings of Syria. Hyrcanus then renewed the friendship originally made by his father with the Romans, who assisted him in being released from the tribute paid to the Syrians; at the same time he received a compensation from them for former injuries done by them to the Jews.

It was at this time that the Edomites, or Idumeans, lived on the south side of Judea. Hyrcanus proposed to them either to embrace Judaism or leave the country. The Edomites readily acquiesced, and became Jews. They ultimately became so incorporated among the Jews, that in less than two centuries scarcely any trace or character was left to signalize the Edomite nation.

Hyrcanus's power being thus increased by the addition of these Edomites, he turned his attention to the Samaritans. He marched with his army and took Shechem, which was then the chief seat of the Samaritan sect; he destroyed their Temple which Sanballat had built for them on Mount Gerizim. The Samaritans, however, continued to keep the altar there, and to offer sacrifices thereon.

Hyrcanus became master of Samaria, ruled in Judea, in Galilee, and in some of the adjacent towns; he proved himself one of the noble princes of his age; he, with great perseverance, preserved both the Jewish church and the state from the power of their enemies, throughout a long and tedious government. He was so highly esteemed among the people, that they believed him to be a prophet, from the fact that he had predicted one or two things which eventually came to pass. He built the castle *Baris* on a rock about fifty cubits high, outside the square of the Temple; this was used as the palace of the Asmonean princes in Jerusalem, and here the sacred robes of the high priest were deposited when they were not in use.

Toward the close of his life, Hyrcanus experienced severe troubles; his claim to the priesthood was questioned by a bold and daring man, one of the Pharisees, of whom we shall speak hereafter in the course of the work, as also of the different other sects which sprang up in those days.

Hyrcanus, supposing that this bold man represented the whole body of the Pharisees, without even inquiring into the matter, immediately renounced the Pharisees, and rashly joined the sect called Sadducees. This hasty conclusion of Hyrcanus, considerably lessened that love and esteem in which the people had previously held him. The Pharisees felt indignant at the conduct of Hyrcanus in this instance; and forgetting all former favors received at his hands, proved very ungrateful toward him. They became arrogant and mutinous, which caused Hyrcanus entirely to desert their party, and even refused to meet them any more. Many civil broils and troubles ensued, which sorely embittered the declining life of Hyrcanus, and he died during the following year.

Hyrcanus had been in office nearly thirty years, during which time his wisdom and counsel at home, and his bravery and conquests abroad, marked his reign one of glory and happiness. The commonwealth recovered more of its glory during his government, than at any other period since the return from Babylon. It is generally supposed that his death was hastened by the troubles which began to surround him.

Hyrcanus had five sons; the eldest, named Aristobulus, succeeded his father as high priest and governor in Judea. He then took upon himself the title of king, which had fallen into disuse since the Babylonish captivity.

Aristobulus did not follow the good example of his noble father. We are informed how he became the murderer of his mother; it having been reported that she laid claim to the government. Three of his brothers he put into close confinement, and the fourth, who was even his favorite, he had put to death owing to a false report being raised that he would oppose him in the government.

Aristobulus now fixed his household and other affairs, according to his own wishes. He then put himself at the head of his army, attacked and subdued the Itureans who lived on the north-east of the land of Galilee. Having the people thus in his power, he compelled them to embrace the Jewish religion, which they did out of fear, and thus became mixed among the people of Israel. In the midst of all these victories, Aristobulus was taken sick and brought to Jerusalem. Antigonus, one of his brothers, acted in his stead.

Aristobulus continued dangerously sick, and there appeared but little hope of his recovery. This being apparent to the king's courtiers, who were jealous of Antigonus, they endeavored to persuade the king that his brother was not faithful to him. In this intrigue they were supported by the queen.

On the return of Antigonus to Jerusalem, he repaired to the Temple, there to return thanks to God for his success, and to pray for the recovery of his sick brother. Whilst thus piously engaged, it was represented to the king that his brother was attempting to usurp the government, which the king too readily received as truth, from the statements previously made to him, and gave orders for his brother to appear in the sick chamber. Antigonus obeyed, and attended in full uniform. The king then desired him to unrobe. This command was given in such a tone, as to assure him that a refusal would be considered as treason, and punished accordingly.

Antigonus retired, much degraded and sorely perplexed as to the cause. The queen, who, we have already noticed was in the conspiracy, then wrote to him that the king had changed his mind and that he wished to see him in his uniform, having been told of the beauty of his armour. Antigonus accordingly repaired in full dress to the palace, and on his way to the king's chamber, he was slain by the guard. This assassination of Antigonus, caused the king to reflect with keen remorse, both on account of this murder, as well as that of his mother. His mind became sorely agitated, which brought on a vomiting of blood, so that he died in great agony of both body and mind.

Thus ended the life of him, who is handed down to posterity as one of the most wretched beings recorded in the annals of Jewish history; and it is worthy of notice how God punishes the wicked. He who had shed so much innocent blood, that his own blood was made to flow from him until he breathed his last; an example as well as a warning to those who were in the service of this wicked man, and who were following the same sinful career as their cruel master.

Aristobulus was succeeded by his brother Alexander; he began his reign by putting his brother to death, because of some attempt to supplant him in the government. Alexander immediately set about arranging all matters relating to the home department, and then commenced to attack his neighbors around him without any reserve.

At this time Ptolemy Lathyrus was heir to the crown of Egypt; Alexander behaved very deceitfully toward him, which caused much enmity and ill feeling to exist on both sides; and the result was, a very severe battle between them, near the river Jordan. Alexander and his army were completely routed, with the loss of about thirty thousand men.

There is a very cruel and barbarous action charged to Lathyrus on this occasion. On the evening after the victory, he marched his men from the field of battle to take up quarters in the adjacent villages, which were all crowded with the wives and children of the vanquished army. He gave orders to kill all of them, without any distinction; their bodies to be cut in pieces and boiled in cauldrons. It is supposed that he did this with a view of creating terror among all the surrounding nations, and to cause a belief that his men fed on human flesh. After this, Lathyrus ranged at liberty all over the country, plundering and destroying it in a very lamentable manner; for Alexander after this battle, was not in a condition to resist him.

In this dilemma, Alexander fortunately met with assistance from Cleopatra, the queen of Egypt. Cleopatra, fearing lest Lathyrus, her eldest son, should become possessed of Judea, and might be induced to take Egypt out of her hands, agreed with her youngest son to support Alexander.

Alexander, encouraged by such offers of support, resumed his courage, besieged many places, and gained the fortress of Gadara and Anathus, toward Galilee, together with much treasure; but he was surprised by Theodorus, prince of Philadelphia, who had laid up that treasure there, with the loss of ten thousand men. Yet being a man of courage and diligence, Alexander assembled his men and succeeded in taking the city of Gaza from the Philistines, who were entirely defeated by his army. He took possession of the chief cities, and made them part of his own dominions. The Philistines being thus subdued, were glad to embrace Judaism as a protection from further inroads. It appears to have now become a custom with the Asmonean princes to impose their religion on all the conquered, leaving them no other choice but to become proselytes or to be banished.

Alexander was not, however, well supported by his own people, many of them being opposed to him. These were chiefly of the Pharisees, who were very numerous and influential, and were supported by a large body of their class, who were excited to such a degree, that they insulted Alexander, while at the altar performing the duties devolving upon him as high priest.

Alexander, enraged at such conduct by his own people, sought to be revenged, and appointed his own body guard from the heathen nations, fearing to trust himself in the hands of his own people. This act brought on a civil war which lasted six years; it was the cause of much grief and calamity throughout the land, and occasioned the death of about fifty thousand people. Though Alexander gained many victories over his enemies, yet he became much weakened from their continual attacks: he at length sued for peace, offering the people to grant them whatever they would reasonably desire. But so embittered were the people against him, that they declared nothing would satisfy them but his life. This reply on their part, aggravated the cause, and the war was continued still more rigorously on both sides. As all mundane affairs must have an end, Alexander after having encountered many severe conflicts, at last gained one great battle, which concluded this protracted war. Numbers of his enemies fell victims to his fury, while others were driven to the city of Bethome, and there were besieged. Alexander having taken the place, he had eight hundred of the people carried to Jerusalem, and there had them all slain in one day, together with their wives and children. This act of Alexander's terrified the Jews to such an extent that they never again attempted any insurrection. We cannot however refrain from observing here, that however provoked Alexander might have been, he justly merited by this cruel conduct the reproach of after ages; such conduct being incompatible with his dignified station as high priest, in whose heart nought but peace and humanity should ever find place.

Alexander, like most cruel monarchs after having satiated their lust for blood, gave himself up to very inordinate luxuries, which in the end produced an attack of ague, very severe in its character. This disease ultimately proved fatal to Alexander, who died in the camp while he was besieging a castle of the Gerasenes beyond Jordan. Alexander reigned twenty-seven years; he left two sons, Hyrcanus and Aristobulus; he bequeathed the government to his wife Alexandra, during her life time, and to be disposed of at her death to which of her sons she pleased. Alexandra in a flood of tears, expressed to her dying husband her justly apprehended dread of the Pharisees, who had grown into a powerful party at that time in Jerusalem. Alexander listened to his wife with considerable emotion, while he employed his last moments in contriving an expedient for the removal of her fears. The dying man then addressed his wife in the following words:

"Alexandra, you are not unacquainted with the cause of our mutual enmity. I am well convinced that your security and happiness, when I am dead, must rise or fall, as you make them your friends or your foes. I advise you, therefore, to keep my death a secret from the army, till they have taken the fort, then lead them in triumph to Jerusalem; carry my body with you, and as soon as you arrive assemble the heads and the leaders of that party, and lay it before them; tell them you submit it wholly to them, after the injuries it had done them, to give it burial, or cast it ignominiously on the highway; as for your part, you are devoted to them, they shall always be your first advisers, at the head of your council; you will do nothing without their consent and approbation; begin instantly to show them some marks of your favor and friendship, upon which they will order my body a royal burial, and they will support you and your sons in the peaceful enjoyment of the kingdom."

Alexandra followed the advice of her husband, and kept his death a secret from the world, till the castle was taken. She then led the army back to Jerusalem, and gave the body of her deceased husband to the Pharisees, to act with it as they pleased, at the same time declared herself ready to be guided by them in the management of all the affairs of the government. This declaration on the part of Alexandra, gained for her the confidence of the Pharisees, who granted to her late husband an honorable funeral.

Alexandra thus enjoying the good opinion of the Pharisees, assumed the government, enlisted herself under their banner, and became firmly and peaceably settled on the throne; she then invested Hyrcanus, her eldest son, with the office of high priest. Alexandra, at the request of a party of the Pharisees, gave her consent to punish all the persons who had counselled her late husband to behave so cruelly to the mass of the people; these men were in their turn put to death by the Pharisees. The queen was induced to adopt this medium in order to prevent any further civil wars; the evil consequences of which she had so sadly experienced, and which, therefore, she was so desirous to avoid.

Alexandra having reigned nine years, died in the seventy-third year of her age; leaving by her will, the whole of the government to her eldest son, Hyrcanus, who was then the high priest. He is known in history by Hyrcanus the second. He was bred and trained in the schools of the Pharisees, and consequently influenced by their tutorage.

Hyrcanus did not long enjoy his new office. Aristobulus, his younger brother, perceiving that the people and the army were weary of the administration of the Pharisees, raised an army against his brother Hyrcanus, and marched them on to the plains of Jericho. A desperate battle was fought, Hyrcanus was put to flight, and the remainder of his forces joined those of Aristobulus. Hyrcanus in this dilemma, went to Jerusalem, shut himself up with a small party in the citadel, and appeared happy to accept any terms in order to procure peace.

Aristobulus then deprived his brother of both the regal and pontifical dignities, commanding the same to be resigned to him, which having been done, Hyrcanus was expelled the capital, and compelled to retire into private life. Hyrcanus, being of a peaceful disposition, made no resistance, although he had enjoyed his regal honors but three months.

Aristobulus then ascended the throne of his father, but he did not prove so happy on it as he had anticipated, as we shall learn from the following circumstance. An Idumean named Antipater, who was brought up in the court of Alexander with Hyrcanus, advised him to seek assistance at the hands of Aretas, the king of Arabia, and not quietly suffer himself to be so easily vanquished. Hyrcanus, acting on the advice of Antipater, applied to

Aretas, who immediately headed an army to espouse the cause of Hyrcanus. An obstinate battle took place in which Aristobulus was totally defeated, driven into the mountains, and there sorely besieged.

At this time there lived at Jerusalem, a very pious man named Onias. He was so much esteemed and beloved by the people for his true piety and virtue, that it was generally believed, that at the instance of this good man's prayers, the Almighty had sent rain from heaven in a season of great drought. The people imagining that he possessed a similar power in cursing as well as blessing, prayed to him to curse Aristobulus and all his party. This good man weary of their importunities, and anxious if possible to satisfy their wishes, raised his hands towards heaven in prayer, of which the following is said to be a copy:

"O God of the universe, since those that are with us are thy people, and they that are besieged in the Temple are thy priests, I pray that thou wouldst hear the prayers of neither of them against each other."

The multitude, disappointed at the good man's prayer, cruelly murdered him on the spot.

This circumstance tended to increase the enmity between both parties, and provoked a warfare between the two brothers and their parties.

The two brothers ultimately agreed with each other to lay the matter before Pompey, the Roman general, for his decision. The mass of the people, however, were not satisfied with this plan of appealing to the Roman general, and declared that they would not be ruled by princes, but by God's priests. The appeal was made to Pompey, who did not feel disposed to give an immediate decision. Aristobulus availed himself of this opportunity, and prepared himself for a fresh war. Pompey hearing this, immediately seized Aristobulus in one of his castles, and confined him in prison. He then marched his army in front of Jerusalem; a division within weakened its power, the two opposite parties contending. At length Hyrcanus's party prevailed and threw open the gates of the city. The adherents to Aristobulus retreated and fortified themselves in the Temple, and on Mount Moriah. Pompey and his army marched through the city, and laid close siege to the Temple. The Jews held out for three months; at length a huge tower was thrown down, and a breach was made large enough for an assault; the place was taken sword in hand, and so fierce was the battle, that more than twelve thousand persons were slain.

It has been remarked by historians, "how is it possible that so strong a place could have been taken in so short a time?" The cause of this easy victory on the part of the Romans was, in consequence of the Jews having suffered the enemy to prepare their war machines on the Sabbath day undisturbed, notwithstanding the agreement made in the days of Judas Maccabees, that they should defend themselves if attacked on the Sabbath day.

Pompey then entered the holy edifice, and being overawed by some religious prepossession, refrained from defiling any of the sacred vessels, nor did he attempt to touch about two thousand talents of gold, which were laid up for the service of God's Holy Temple. On the contrary, Pompey ordered the Temple to be purified, and on the very next day, its usual services were resumed. Thus an end was put to the very serious quarrel and contention between the two brothers.

It may be worthy of notice, that though this Roman general was not disposed to plunder the sacred property of the Temple on this occasion, yet it escaped not the avarice and covetousness of another Roman general. Crassus, when he became Governor of Judea instead of Gabinius, plundered the Temple, and carried off the solid beams of gold, magnificent vessels, utensils and golden tables, and all the beautiful hangings, which adorned the Holy of Holies. This wicked man's sacrilege did not pass unpunished, for when he was in an engagement with the Parthians, he was defeated, and met with his death, and as a mark of infamy, his head was cut off, and molten gold was poured down his throat, to show to the people how much benefit the gold was to him which he took from the holy Temple.

Pompey now demolished the walls of Jerusalem, slew many of the chief supporters of Aristobulus, and restored Hyrcanus to the office of high priest, and made him also the Governor, but under tribute to the Romans.

Aristobulus and his sons were carried prisoners to Rome, whence they escaped after a time, and made several attempts to regain their former position, but without success.

It may fairly be concluded that in consequence of the civil broils between Aristobulus and his brother Hyrcanus, the Jewish nationality became very much shaken, and ultimately produced the total ruin of both Jerusalem and the whole of Judea. At this time the regal power was arrested, and enjoyed by the Romans. The sovereign authority had hitherto descended with the priesthood; although at different periods already mentioned, the Jews were subject to the several strange powers who had become their masters.

The enemies of the Jews did not seem to be satisfied with their already degraded state; but every exertion must be made to crush them still more, by even preventing them from attending and praying to the God of their fathers. This infliction appears to have been far more grievous to the nation at large, than all the worldly persecutions which could possibly have been invented against them.

After a short time, Gabinius, a Roman general, passed through Judea on an expedition. He took upon himself to reduce the power of Hyrcanus, and made new arrangements relating to the Sanhedrim or Jewish Senate.

All these differences were however, very happily settled in a short time by Julius Cæsar, who, when Emperor of Rome, listened to the petition of Hyrcanus, and granted him permission to rebuild the walls of Jerusalem. This enabled Hyrcanus to resume the former friendship between the Jews and the Romans, who passed a unanimous decree in their favor.

During this time, Antipater, who had encouraged Hyrcanus in the recovery of the government of Judea, was in the employ of Julius Cæsar. Antipater was appointed Lieutenant of Judea, by Julius Cæsar, under Hyrcanus, who was now in full power both in the government and the priesthood. The eldest son of Antipater was made Governor of Jerusalem, while his second son Herod, was made Governor of Judea. This Herod became after a time, great in power, as we shall hereafter read of him. He was called Herod the Great, and became King of Judea. Antipater did not long enjoy his office. Malichus, who envied him his position, had Antipater poisoned. Herod having discovered this, obtained permission of the Roman general to have Malichus captured and put to death as a murderer.

Pacorus, the Parthian general, was at this time at war with the Romans. By some treachery or other, Hyrcanus, and his eldest son Phasael, came into the custody of Pacorus; Jerusalem was taken, and Antigonus appointed Ruler in Judea. Hyrcanus and his son were delivered over to him in chains and made prisoners. Herod, however, had made his escape. Phasael, weary of his existence in prison, put an end to his own life. Hyrcanus had both his ears lopped off, in order to disqualify him for the priesthood; he was then banished the country to prevent him appearing against Antigonus.

Herod, in the mean time, repaired to Rome, to lodge his complaint, and fully to report all that had happened. Herod was well received by Mark Antony and Octavius, who governed Rome at that time, owing to the death of Julius Cæsar, who was slain in the Senate House at Rome.

Herod's report having been properly accredited, he was immediately appointed King of Judea, by full consent of the Roman Senate.

CHAPTER X.

Of the Government of Herod the Great and his posterity over Israel.

Herod, having received his appointment, returned to Judea. The first thing which engaged his attention, was the releasing of his mother, who had been imprisoned by Antigonus. Herod now declared war against Antigonus, and with the assistance of the Roman legions, he besieged Antigonus in Jerusalem.

While preparations were being made to carry on the siege, Herod went to Samaria, and there married Mariamne, the grand-daughter of Hyrcanus the second, a descendant of the valiant and noble race of the Asmoneans. Mariamne was a lady of exquisite beauty and great virtue, and thus highly calculated to dignify the lofty position she was about to fill as a queen in Israel. She inherited all the piety and goodness of her ancestors, who were justly esteemed ornaments to the Jewish nation. Herod, sensible of this, was the more anxious for the alliance, in the hope of endearing himself to the great body of the people.

Herod, successful in his suit, returned to the siege at Jerusalem, and took it by storm after six months' hard struggle. Antigonus was taken prisoner by the Romans, who sent him to Antioch; he was afterwards put to death by Mark Antony, at the instance of Herod the Great.

The death of Antigonus concluded the race of the Maccabees, who had held the government about one hundred and twenty years.

The possession of Jerusalem, together with the death of Antigonus, established Herod upon the Jewish throne.

Herod commenced his reign in bloodshed, as the only way open to establish himself. The partizans of Antigonus fell easy victims to Herod's cruelty. These were all the counselors of the great Sanhedrim, excepting the two celebrated and learned divines and disputants, Hillel and Shamai. These two influential men induced the people to receive Herod as their King, not for the love they entertained for him, but, because they foresaw the mischief which would have resulted from any opposition on their part. Herod now appointed one Ananelus, a descendant of the house of Aaron as the high priest. He was not of very high rank, but rather of obscure origin, trained far off in Babylon; he was therefore suited for Herod, as not likely to oppose any of his designs which he might form in Judea.

Mariamne, the wife of Herod, considering that the priesthood belonged to her family, prevailed on her husband to remove Ananelus, and place her brother in his stead. The queen's brother was at this time only seventeen years of age; still, he was appointed high priest by Herod, because of his wife's importunities, though much against his own will.

Hyrcanus, who was in banishment among the Parthians during many years, hearing of the advancement of Herod, and his marriage with his grand-daughter, felt a desire to return to Jerusalem, anticipating a kind welcome at the hands of Herod, on account of the family alliance which now so closely united them.

Hyrcanus, arriving at Jerusalem, was received by Herod with all the appearance of pleasure and satisfaction. But a short time after, Herod fancied that Hyrcanus, being of the Asmonean family, might one day or other, take the kingdom from him, although Hyrcanus was now upwards of eighty years old! Herod therefore invented some pretext, and had the old Hyrcanus put to death.

About this season, a very alarming earthquake shook the whole country of Judea, and destroyed about thirty thousand of the inhabitants, together with their houses and their property. Shortly after, a very destructive pestilence infested Judea, and swept away many of the people. A few years later a grievous famine pervaded the land, on which occasion Herod behaved very liberally to the people, in order to gain their affections; but in this he was disappointed.

It was just at this period that Mark Antony and Octavius, the two brave Romans, fell into a disagreement with each other. The result proved in favor of Octavius, by whom Mark Antony was vanquished and entirely ruined.

Mark Antony was the true and tried friend of Herod, who being now fearful of the power of Octavius, sought to appease him by making a servile submission to him. Herod accordingly waited on Octavius in humble attire, having laid aside his royal diadem, and with a free and open countenance, confessed his sincere regard and friendship for Mark Antony in former days; but now he wished to declare his perfect obedience to the will and wishes of Octavius, if such trust would be reposed in him at his hands.

Octavius, allured by the flattery and cringing tone of Herod, received his declaration of obedience in the most polite manner, and requested him immediately to return, resume the crown, and ascend the throne. He then fully established Herod in his kingdom, and remained his friend during his life-time.

The history of Herod's life will be found overshadowed by crimes of the blackest dye. Avarice, envy, jealousy and pride; these had so great an effect upon his wicked mind and cruel heart, that no redeeming quality existed in the breast of this hateful tyrant.

Herod was now visited by severe domestic troubles, which disturbed his peace of mind, and produced in him great irritability of temper, violent grief and rage throughout the remainder of his life.

It will be recollected that Mariamne was one of the most beautiful women in Judea. Herod, fearful lest at his death any other man should possess so great a beauty as his queen, and lest any branch of the Asmonean family should become master of Judea, and thus deprive his own lawful heirs of their right to the crown, gave secret instructions, that if his death should be before that of Mariamne, that both she and her mother should be immediately put to death.

This cruel and inhuman decree of Herod reached the ears of the Queen, who from that very day rejected him for ever, and upbraided him with the murder of her relations, and that by such means alone he had obtained the crown. She further resented his wicked designs, by heaping bitter reproaches on his mother and sister, in reference to the obscurity of their birth and parentage. Herod's conscience becoming tormented, he implored his Queen by all kind and affectionate importunities, but without effect. Mariamne seemed resolved to punish Herod for his wicked intentions. She would not yield to his entreaties, and positively determined to discard him for ever. This conduct of the Queen so enraged Herod, that acting on the advice of his mother and sister Salome, he slew his beautiful and innocent Mariamne, and to palliate this outrageous cruelty, alleged that she had attempted to poison him, and that he only acted in self defense. It was not long before the mother shared the same fate as her daughter at the hands of her relentless son-in-law. The death of Mariamne was not easily forgotten by Herod. It preyed on his mind so violently, that he became one of the most miserable wretches in existence. His love for his Queen whom he had so atrociously put to death, produced extreme grief and vexation of spirit which rendered him truly wretched. He became more arbitrary and despotic in his government; he appointed those whom he wished to favor, as high priests, and deposed them as frequently, to satisfy his unruly passions and caprice of temper.

He introduced innovations into the religious observances of the Temple, in direct opposition to the will of the people, who remonstrated with him on the mischief which would result therefrom.

Notwithstanding all the arguments advanced to dissuade him from such wicked and impious conduct, Herod obstinately adopted the practices and customs of the heathen nations, under the false pretext of pleasing and gratifying the wishes of Cæsar.

Herod's conduct in this respect, brought upon him the hatred of the people; who being jealous at all times lest their ancient and holy religion should in any way be infringed upon, regarded him with suspicious distrust. Herod becoming sensible at last of the disrepute into which he had fallen, and fearful of the consequences thereof, sought to protect himself by building several strong towers in and about Jerusalem. He then built temples in the different places and dedicated them to Cæsar, who was at that time his great friend.

Herod finding that the hatred of the people toward him did not abate, then sought to appease them, by proposing to pull down the old Temple and build up a new one in its stead, far superior in every degree to the one then in existence. In order to induce the people to second his views, he pointed out the necessity of a new Temple, since the old one had undergone many repairs, owing to the frequent outrages which had been committed against it.

The people were, however, not disposed to listen to Herod's proposal to remove the old Temple until he had assured them that it should remain untouched till all the requisites for the new building should be ready and prepared to be set up. Herod, being on this occasion, earnest in his intentions, executed all that the people requested of him, at an enormous outlay of both labor and material. To carry out his plans he employed nearly ten thousand of the best mechanics under the direction of about one thousand priests. At the expiration of two years, the new Temple rose in all its glory and splendor, at an immense labor and cost, as fully described by the faithful historian Josephus, who says it was one of the most magnificent and beautiful structures that ever adorned the country of Judea.

When completed, the Temple was dedicated for divine worship on the anniversary day of Herod's ascension to the throne. The occasion was celebrated with a large number of sacrifices after the ancient custom, and amidst great rejoicings and public festivities.

It has been asked why this new Temple, built by Herod, was not called the third Temple? The reply is, that though it was built anew from the foundation, yet it was only by way of reparation, it not having been destroyed by the enemy as in the days of Nebuchadnezzar; nor did it lay in ashes, and remain desolate, as the first Temple. It is therefore still designated by the name of the second Temple.

Herod having completed this work to the satisfaction of the people, was anxious to further secure their good opinion; he therefore procured for such of his people who were scattered in Greece and Asia Minor, a renewal of their privileges, and permission to live in other countries, according to their own laws and religion, which had been granted them before by the kings of Syria, and by the Romans.

Herod was not permitted to enjoy that peace of mind which he anticipated; he was visited with domestic troubles which he little expected, but which he richly deserved. Aristobulus and Alexander, the two eldest sons of Mariamne, who were educated at Rome, now returned to Jerusalem. These youths deeply lamented the loss of their mother, and often reflected with sorrow on her untimely death, and they gave vent to their feelings by public demonstrations of their resentment for the death of their injured parent. These expressions being repeatedly and loudly declared, were very disagreeable to the ears of Salome, the sister of Herod, who was instrumental in the death of Mariamne. Salome being wickedly disposed, and probably fearing the vengeance of the two youths, endeavored to rouse the jealousy and anger of Herod against his sons, by persuading him that they were plotting against his life. This intelligence created disputes and quarrels between the father and the two sons, which lasted many years, and caused Herod much annoyance and fear during the remainder of his old age. Salome, by her crafty design, ultimately succeeded in effecting the execution of the two sons by an edict from Herod, and the sanction to the same at the hands of Augustus Cæsar. It must be observed that Herod had been already married to one Doris, previous to his alliance with Mariamne. By this wife he had a son named Antipater, who had been actively engaged with Salome in procuring the death of the two sons of this said Herod.

When Herod was displeased with his two sons, he placed Antipater in some post of honor; and now that they were dead, he intended that Antipater should succeed in the kingdom. Antipater eager to obtain the crown, conspired to poison his father. This being detected, he was sentenced and condemned to be executed, by and under the directions of Augustus Cæsar, and with Herod's approbation. This was the third son whom Herod put to death. In the seventieth year of his age, and five days after the death of Antipater, Herod himself died by a dreadful complication of diseases. He was attacked by fever and ulcerated bowels, in which excruciating pain he lingered for some time, till he died. No doubt the extreme pains which he suffered, were inflicted as a punishment for his enormous cruelties, and the multiplied iniquities of his whole life.

On his death-bed, Herod, considering that the extreme hatred the people had for him would prevent them from lamenting his loss, and that his death would no doubt cause much rejoicing in the land, was determined even in his last moments to be wicked and cruel. To effect this, he convened a meeting of all the principal Jews, from all parts of the kingdom, on pain of death, to appear at Jericho where he then lay. He ordered them all to be shut up prisoners, and then commanded his sister Salome and her husband, his chief confidants, that they should have them all put to the sword by the soldiery, for this, said he, "will provide mourners for my funeral all over the land."

Herod died, but his orders were not attended to, for Salome, although wicked, hesitated to commit so horrid a deed as the murder of so many innocent persons, and therefore as soon as Herod was dead, she released all the prisoners.

At Herod's death, his son Archelaus succeeded him in the government of Judea, nearly ten years, during which time he was guilty of many acts of cruelty and tyranny, for which he was ultimately deposed by the Roman emperor, and banished to an obscure place in France. The Romans being so displeased with the evil practices and bad government of Archelaus, they reduced Judea to a Roman province, to be ruled by a Roman procurator or governor, who was sent thither and removed therefrom at pleasure. It was now that the power of life and death was taken out of the hands of the Jews, and placed in that of the Roman governor; and from that time all taxes were gathered by the publicans, and paid directly to the Roman emperor.

This new regulation very much annoyed the people; for the Pharisees, and all those under their influence, considering it unlawful to acknowledge a heathen for their king or governor, looked upon their tax-gatherers with greater detestation than any of those kings or governors of former days, appointed to rule over them, and who were of their own nation or religion. True, Herod was an Idumean by birth, yet all the Idumeans having embraced the Jewish religion, he was so far counted a lawful governor, that the people did not scruple to pay him their taxes. The Romans followed the plan adopted by Herod in the appointment of the high priests, and the removing of them as often as they pleased, to answer their own purposes.

In this way the affairs of the Jews were carried on for some years, when about this period christianity was ushered into the world; which caused much rage and persecution to take place among the Jews, until at last they were driven to such extremities, and thus exposed to the furious and formidable army of the Romans, who were then great in power; and the Jews were thus so weakened by the continued inroads made upon them, that they fell an easy prey to the enemy. The city of Jerusalem was utterly demolished, the beautiful Temple desecrated and finally destroyed, and about eleven hundred of the people perished in the conflict. The country all round became desolate; the streets overflowing with human blood, terrified the few of the poor Jews who still survived, so that they fled for their lives, and were scattered all over the face of the globe. Thus ended the Jewish polity; from that time up to the present, the Jewish nation has been dispersed throughout the known world; seeking protection under those governments where they may chance to fix their residence. In concluding this portion of the work, we venture the following few remarks:

From the time when the Jews returned from the Babylonish captivity, both the Temple service and the general affairs of the nation at large, appear to have been in an unsettled state. Oppressed and persecuted by the various powers near and about Judea; the continued civil broils among themselves; the tyranny and cruelty of their own kings and priests, all tended to keep them in a state of confusion and disorder: yet worse still, was the neglect of God's holy laws, and the introduction of heathen rites and customs, by which the pure religion of their ancestors became polluted. Add to this the innovations which were permitted to creep in upon the sacred worship of God, and the party feeling which strengthened such on the one hand, and the furious opposition on the other—this had the effect of preventing the nation from possessing that peace of mind and happiness which they would have otherwise enjoyed, owing to those glorious prophetic predictions which made such an impression on them, and which promised nought but real comfort and divine peace on their release from Babylonish captivity.

It is therefore to be concluded that there is a period yet to come, which shall bring together again all the scattered flock of Israel, to the Holy Land of their fathers. Then will they be convinced of their past errors, and the sins committed by their fathers of old, whose wickedness brought down upon them the just vengeance of an offended God. Then will all the blessings reserved for the righteous, be conferred upon them in that day, as foretold by the prophet Zephaniah:

"At that time will I bring you *again*, even in the time that I gather you; for I will make you a name and a praise among all the people of the earth, when I turn back your captivity before your eyes, saith the Lord."

END OF PART I.

Part Second.

AN ACCOUNT OF THE SEVERAL SECTS WHICH SPRANG UP AMONG THE JEWS BEFORE AND AFTER THE DAYS OF THE MACCABEES.

CHAPTER I.

The Assideans.

After the spirit of prophecy had ceased among the Jews, and there being no inspired persons to whom they could apply as formerly, they fell into religious doubts and disputes. This caused different opinions to exist among them, and divided them into sects and parties; such as the Pharisees, the Sadducees, and the Essenes, who were the principal, and supposed to have arisen out of the Assideans.

The Assideans are called by some "Chasidim," or *pious*. They were a religious society among the Jews, whose chief and distinguishing character appears to have been to support the honor of the Temple, and observe punctually the traditions of the Elders. In the apocryphal books of the Maccabees, we meet with the word "asidaioi," which no doubt is derived from the Hebrew word *chasidim*. This sect is supposed to date their origin either during the captivity, or shortly after the restoration of the nation. Being of a pious and religious character, they were the first who adhered to Mattathias, and afterwards to his son Judas Maccabees, in defense of their religion and the Law of God. They proved themselves zealous in their cause, as stated in the following passage: "There came to Mattathias, a company of Assideans, who were mighty men of Israel, even all such as were voluntarily devoted unto the law." They were not however, considered a distinct religious sect from the rest of their brethren; but they were devoted to their ancient religion and the service of the Temple, the supporting of the sacrifices, the relief of the poor, and the general benefit of all their co-religionists. Our views on the subject may be considered correct, as Josephus, who wrote in those times, and concerning those affairs, does not mention any such sect being distinctly marked from the general body of the people. We may therefore safely adopt the opinions of those who consider the appellation given them in the book of the Maccabees, to be no more than used in our days to pious and religious men, who are designated saints or holy men.

CHAPTER II.

The Pharisees.

This sect derived their name from the Hebrew word "Perusheem," which signifies separation, and so called because of their being separated from the body of the people in point of their religious conduct. They considered themselves more than ordinarily holy, and more strict in the observance of their religious precepts and ceremonies. It is not quite certain at what time the Pharisees first made their appearance; yet there is no doubt, that like all the other sects among the Jews, they were not known in any way, until some time after the death of Malachi, the last of the prophets, when the spirit of prophecy ceased to exist among Israel. Josephus, who was himself of this sect, speaks of it as flourishing in the days of Johnathan the high priest. In the days of John Hyrcanus, a high priest of the Asmonean race, they became very numerous and influential. It is generally admitted that the Pharisees were more devout than their brethren, and appear to have excelled in the knowledge of the law, and to have been more skillful in their interpretation of the same.

The principal doctrines of this sect were as follows:

They held sacred all the traditions of the elders in those days, and considered the laws of the Rabbins, as contained in the said traditions, equally binding upon them as the written law. They were of the belief that the written law could not be properly understood without the explanation of the oral law, which removed the apparent difficult passages in the written law. They were guided by the conviction that both were derived from the same fountain, as handed down by the tradition from father to son. They further believed, that when Moses was with God on the mount during forty days, he received from him both laws—the one in writing, the other traditionary, which contained the sense and explanation of the former. That Moses having returned to his tent, taught the same to Aaron, then to his sons, afterwards to the seventy elders, and lastly to all the people. That the same was further continued throughout every generation until their day, and that consequently they considered their system the only true one, in order to the understanding of the law and the performance of its precepts. This sect became the most numerous of all the others, since their doctrines were supported by the scribes and expounders of the law, who were the most competent judges in those days, and hence the best calculated to guide the people in all their religious duties.

The Pharisees were, therefore, much respected and highly esteemed by the general class of the people, who followed their example in the performance of all their religious observances, and because they would not encourage any innovations to be made in their religion or temple worship. They were very particular in the performance of all the ceremonial part of their religion, considering form and custom to be the great contributing cause to the cementing more firmly the principles upon which the Jewish religion is based, and that frequent changes in religious affairs tend materially to weaken, but not to strengthen, the cause.

They maintained the belief in the resurrection of the body—at least of the good—and the future rewards and punishments to all men in an eternal state of retribution, believing that every soul is immortal. They ascribed some things to fate, but held that other things were left in man's own power; that all things were decreed by divine power, yet not so as to take away the freedom of man in the discharge of those duties which he is expected to perform in this life, in order to obtain the promised happiness of an hereafter.

The religion of the Jew in the present day, is that which was practised by the sect called Pharisees, and is in general use among all the descendants of Israel, wherever they may be dispersed throughout the earth. There are some few exceptions, in those who have seceded, and have set up a standard for themselves; but they are few in number, and not very significant in the scale of Judaism. The principle which they so strenuously advocate is a mere change in the formulæ of prayer, and the mode of synagogue worship, under the idea of conciliating the Gentiles, by whom they are surrounded. The belief in the coming of the Messiah, and the resurrection of the dead, as also the restoration of Israel to the promised land, is not in the least invalidated. The Jews in general look forward with anxious hope for the forthcoming of that period in which all this shall come to pass, as so frequently foretold by the prophets in the various ages in which they flourished.

CHAPTER III.

The Sadducees.

The Sadducees derive their name from the Hebrew word "Tzaddukeem," so called from Zadok, who was a pupil of Antigonus, the son of Socho, president of the Sanhedrim, upwards of two thousand years ago. This sect arose from the following circumstance.

Antigonus taught in his school the doctrine that "Man ought to serve God from pure love, and not in a servile manner, either out of fear of punishment or the hope of reward."

Zadok, not comprehending the spiritual idea of this doctrine, concluded that there would not be any future state of reward or punishment; and, accordingly, taught and propagated this false doctrine after the death of his preceptor, Antigonus.

This sect believed in the written law as handed down from the time of Moses; but not in the oral or traditional law. They rejected all the traditions maintained among the Pharisees. They not only denied the resurrection of the body, but even the existence of the soul after its departure from the body here on earth. They ignored the idea entertained of divine decrees, and held the belief that man is absolute master of his own actions, with the full privilege of acting as he pleases, either for good or evil. That God does not in anywise influence his creatures in the doing the one or the other; that man's prosperity or adversity in life depends entirely on his own acts, and that both are respectively the result of either his wisdom or his folly. The Sadducees received the Pentateuch as divine; but not the other books of the old testament. In the days of Josephus, the celebrated Jewish historian, the Sadducees were not very numerous, but supposed to have been the most wealthy among the people; and the more opulent joined them. We can easily reconcile this to our minds, as we observe in our times that the rich and the great are apt to prefer the pleasures and enjoyments of this life to any expectancy in a future state of existence. Hence they are found ready and willing to embrace such a system of religion as enables them to follow their own inclinations.

These men do not wish to tax their minds with any uneasy reflections on the subject of retribution, or of the world to come, when they shall be called to account for their past conduct in this life.

The Sadduccees were, however, not tolerated among the mass of the people, in consequence of their assertions, precepts, and doctrines, which were held by the community at large as impious, and, therefore, injurious to the happiness of society.

At the destruction of Jerusalem, this sect became very insignificant—their name became nearly forgotten for many years—and subsequently the name was applied to the sect called Karaites, whom we shall notice hereafter, in reproach and disgrace.

CHAPTER IV.

The Samaritans.

The Samaritans were originally heathens, consisting of persons from the several nations, to whom the king of Assyria gave the lands and cities of the Israelites when they were made captives by the said monarch.

This sect was called Samaritans from the fact of their having been settled in the city of Samaria, the metropolis of the kingdom of Israel. When these people were first carried to Samaria, they adopted the idolatrous worship and customs of the surrounding nations from among whom they came.

History informs us that Samaria was infested with lions, which the people supposed to be a judgment from heaven for their idolatrous and superstitious practices.

The king of Assyria being of the same opinion with the rest of the people, sent a Jewish priest to instruct them in the Jewish religion, and to put away their idolatry.

Notwithstanding the instruction they received from the Jewish priest, these people could not easily be weaned from their old practices; and, therefore, to conciliate all parties, as they supposed, they made up among themselves a system embracing the principles of both the Jewish and the heathen religion.

At the return of the Jewish nation from the Babylonish captivity—and after the rebuilding of the temple at Jerusalem—the religion of the Samaritans underwent a revision, and an alteration in many points, under the following extraordinary circumstances.

One of the sons of Jehoiada, the high priest, married the daughter of Sanballat, the Horonite, contrary to the Mosaical law, which prohibits the inter-marriage of the Israelite with any of the other nations.

Nehemiah in his day zealously endeavored to reform the people among whom this innovation had spread itself to an alarming extent. He compelled all those men who had married strange women to repudiate them.

Manasseh, unwilling to obey the order of Nehemiah, together with many others who acted in concert with him, left Jerusalem with their wives, and settled themselves under the protection of Sanballat, the governor of Samaria.

From that time onward, the worship of the Samaritans came much nearer to that of the Jews. At a later date, they obtained permission from Alexander the Great, to build a temple on Mount Gerizim, near the city of Samaria, in imitation of the temple at Jerusalem, where they followed the same system of worship, with some few exceptions.

This sect bears some affinity to the Sadducees—it being the prevailing opinion among the learned, that they rejected all other sacred writings excepting the five books of Moses.

This circumstance created a strong hatred between the Samaritans and the original Jews. It was considered in those days a great reproach among the Jews to be designated a Samaritan. So violent was the animosity on both sides, that the one would not in any way associate with the other, nor even perform any acts of civility to each other, and thus all friendly intercourse ceased among them.

The Samaritans, as well as the Sadducees, are sometimes called by the Jewish Rabbins, "Cutheem."

CHAPTER V.

The Essenes.

This sect is supposed to have first appeared a short time before the days of the Maccabees, when the faithful among the Jews, at least those who were the most scrupulously religious, had to flee from the power of their cruel enemies, and take up their abode in the deserts and in caves. Living in such retreats, many of them became so habituated to retirement, that they preferred to remain so even in later days, when they might have again appeared in public. In this way it was, that they formed themselves into recluses.

Although this sect has not been noticed in the scripture history of the Jews, still they formed a considerable party among them, as mentioned by Josephus. The Essenes appear to have been rather peculiar in their mode of living. They loved to be in solitude and retirement, and were devoted to a contemplative life. They were singular in their piety, humility, and devotion. It is supposed by some of the ancient writers, that among this sect it was that the Hebrew philosophy and metaphysics chiefly flourished, because they showed but little regard for worldly pleasures—as wealth, honors, or vain-glories. They were remarkable for their patience, moral conduct, and for their strict observance of the Sabbath according to the law of Moses.

They were exemplary in their manner of worship, for they would not speak of any worldly affairs after the sun had risen, until they had performed their religious duties as customary in those days. In the present day, nothing is known of this sect; the probability is, that in the lapse of time, they became mixed up among the rest of their brethren in their various dispersions throughout the world.

From the account given of the doctrines of this sect by Philo and Josephus, that they believed in the immortality of the soul; that they held the scripture in great reverence; they offered no sacrifices, but sent presents for the support of the temple at Jerusalem.

Their quiet, pious habits, rendered them remarkable. They remained neutral amidst all the political changes, and were thus respected by all parties of their own nation, as well as those of the heathens. They lived chiefly in Palestine and in Egypt.

CHAPTER VI.

The Herodians.

The Herodians were considered by some to be a political party, and by others, a religious sect. Josephus appears to have passed over this sect in silence, which leads us to suppose that he did not consider them very formidable. The opinion, however, of most ecclesiastics, is, that they derived their name from Herod the Great, and that they were distinguished from the Pharisees, and other Jews, by their agreeing with Herod's scheme in putting himself and his dominions under the power of the Romans, and complying with many of the heathen usages and customs.

In their zeal for the Roman authority, they were directly opposite to the Pharisees, who considered it unlawful to submit to, or to pay taxes to, the Roman emperor. The Pharisees encouraged this opinion, because they were forbidden by the law of Moses to set over them a stranger to be their king. The Herodians were also distinguished, having adopted some of the idolatrous worship of the heathens, which had been introduced among them by Herod the Great, when he built a temple in honor of Cæsar, near the head of the river Jordan; and erected a magnificent theatre at Jerusalem, in which he introduced the pagan games, and placed the figure of a golden eagle over the gate of the holy temple.

Herod also furnished the temples, which he reared in the several places out of Judea, with images for idolatrous worship, in order to gain favor with the emperor of Rome; though, at the same time, to the Jews he pretended to do it in opposition to his own will, but in obedience to the imperial ordinance. In all these schemes the Herodians acquiesced, and encouraged their master in his work of iniquity.

It is also probable, from some account in ancient history, that the Herodians were chiefly of the sect of the Sadducees, who were very lax in the performance of their religious duties. This sect was, however, after a very few years, lost in oblivion, and up to the present day, nothing more is known of them.

CHAPTER VII.

The Galileans, or Gaulonites.

A sect among the ancient Jews, so called from their founder or leader, Judas of Galilee. It is supposed that this party seceded from the Pharisees, and formed themselves into a new sect.

This Judas, considering it to be improper for his countrymen to pay tribute to strangers, excited them to oppose the edict of the emperor, Augustus, who had decreed that a census should be taken of all his subjects.

He declared his reason for this opposition to be, that God alone should be honored as the supreme master, and not any earthly monarch. This Judas was in company with one Zadoc, a Sadducee, and they publicly taught that such taxation was forbidden by the law of Moses. The tumults which they excited were, however, for a time suppressed; but their disciples were active in propagating this doctrine. This caused a secession from the body of the Pharisees, declaring it to be unlawful to pay for infidel princes. In all other respects, they held the same doctrine as the original Pharisees; but apart from them, they performed the duties of sacrifices, and all other forms of worship peculiar among them in those days.

It is generally supposed that this sect of Galileans ultimately embodied among themselves most of the other sects which appeared at that time; and it is even credited, that the zealots, particularly mentioned at the siege of Jerusalem, were of this faction.

CHAPTER VIII.

The Karayeem, or Karaites.

The Karaites trace their pedigree from the ten tribes who were carried away captive by Salmanassar, and settled themselves in Tartary. They derive their name from the word Kara, which signifies scripture, they having adhered to the scripture only as the rule of their faith and religion. Hence they were called Karayeem. They reject the Talmud and the Mishna, as also all other traditions, and confine themselves strictly to the written law—the word of God, as they term it—and content themselves with the literal sense of the text, which admits of no comment, according to their opinions. The translation of the bible in use among them, is in the Turkish language, which in all probability proceeds from their constant intercourse with the Mahomedans.

During the time of the celebrated Hillel, and his cotemporary, Shammai, who were the president and vice president of the Sanhedrin of those days, the disciples of these two eminent divines became divided, and formed two parties. They were in constant disputes, owing to the different opinions entertained by each party on the several religious subjects. Those who were of the same opinion as the Karaites, agreed with the school of Shammai; whilst those who were zealous advocates for tradition, joined the school of Hillel. Though the name Karaites be thus modern, this sect boasts of their high antiquity; for they say they are the true followers of Moses and the prophets, as they undoubtedly are, on account of their adhering so closely to the scripture.

This sect differs from the rest of the Jews in this respect—they expound the scripture, after its having been read in the synagogue in Hebrew, in the language of the country in which they dwell; and they read most of their prayers after the same manner, both in private and in public. At Constantinople, where many of them are living, their translation is in modern Greek; whereas, in Caffa, it is in the Turkish language. They are found chiefly in the Crimea, Lithuania, and Persia, at Damascus, Constantinople, and Egypt.

They are proverbial for honesty and integrity, and said to be men of great learning, piety, and true religious principles.

Their doctrines chiefly are as follow:

They believe in the immortality of the soul, and in rewards and punishments hereafter. They believe, also, with the rest of Israel, that the Messiah is yet to come, with the same hope and fervency of spirit as all Jews of the present day.

They are exemplary in their observance of the Sabbath, and the festivals, according to the strict letter of the law, as contained in the bible.

The celebrated traveler, Benjamin of Tudela, who made himself famous in the twelfth century, visited all the synagogues in the east, where he became acquainted with all the customs, manners, and ceremonies of the different parties. He relates that he met some Karaites at Damascus, in Syria, and in Egypt; that they all appear to have adopted one uniform mode of worship and religious practices; that they met with great encouragement in the Ottoman empire, owing to their unanimity of feeling in synagogue worship, and their general conduct in religious affairs. In Constantinople, where they are pretty numerous, they hold an equal position. It was here that Elijah ben Moses composed his astronomical tables for the capital of the Ottoman empire. It was here, also, that the learned Rabbi, Judah Alpoka, the noted Karaite, published his work, the "Gate of Judah," in which he deplores the unfortunate state of his sect, which, he says, had lost, by plunder and other persecution, about three hundred volumes of books, composed in Arabic by their doctors, and translated into Hebrew.

This historian further informs us, that this sect is to be found in Syria, and as far to the east as Nineveh, from which place, some years ago, one of the Karaites came to Frankfort, in Germany. He brought with him some books, which he valued at a very high price. He then visited Poland, Muscovy, and Lithuania, where many of them are residing at this day. This proves to us the folly of the vulgar notion, that this sect are extinct in the west. Doubtless, there are still many Karaites in these countries who trace their origin from the Tartars.

Our historian further informs us that, in the course of his travels, he met in Damascus two hundred Karaites, four hundred Samaritans, and about three thousand Pharisees, and that none of these sects would intermarry; and consequently, they remain to this day distinct and separate, so far as regards their religious intercourse and forms of worship. In all other respects, however, they are friendly with each other, and mix together in society as citizens of the world.

CHAPTER IX.

Of the Synagogues among the Jews.

The term synagogue signifies simply an assemblage of persons, which name was applied to places or houses in which the people met for religious worship. Among the Israelites of old, the word synagogue was used in its primary sense; as when they speak of the great synagogue, or the court of the seventy elders, which was instituted in the days of Moses, the legislator, to superintend the political affairs of the nation. The number of seventy became, in later days, increased to one hundred and twenty.

Synagogues were originally instituted as chapels of ease, for the convenience of those persons who lived far distant from the temple, and could not, therefore, attend regularly to divine service. In the later ages of the Jewish state, synagogues became very numerous, even in Jerusalem, where the temple stood.

The silence of the old testament respecting synagogues, and the absence of any other authentic account, have induced most historians to conclude that synagogues were not generally in use before the Babylonish captivity.

It appears to be the current opinion of many who have written on the subject, that synagogues were first built during the days of Ezra and Nehemiah. They directed that in every town and city throughout the land, where ten men could be assembled, synagogues should be erected for divine worship, which consisted of prayers and praises, reading the scripture, and expounding the same, in the language of the country in which the people lived.

The Israelites having, during their long captivity in Babylon, neglected the study of the Hebrew language, which was their vernacular, the result proved that the bible became less understood by them. It was on this account that Ezra read the law to the people in Hebrew, and the meaning of the text was given in Chaldee by the Levites; and thus it was, that the people were enabled to comprehend the true and proper meaning of that portion of the law when read publicly every Sabbath in the synagogue. Hence the origin of preaching in the synagogue, which was considered one of the objects for which the synagogue was instituted.

After the Babylonish captivity, the erection of synagogues among the Israelites proved of great utility to the people in general, as the frequent public reading of the law was the only means of preserving the true religion of the Jew, and of diffusing the knowledge of the holy law of God. It cannot be denied, that it had been partially forgotten during the long and severe captivity; that many of the rites and ceremonies had fallen into disuse, in consequence of the many cruel persecutions which were inflicted upon the people, which unfitted them for the performance of God's holy law.

The regulations for divine service were as follow. Two days in each week, besides the Sabbath and other festivals, were appointed for this service in the synagogue, viz: Mondays and Thursdays. The hours for the daily prayers were at the time of the morning and evening sacrifices. These hours were devoted to prayer in the temple as well as in the synagogues, as also to private devotion in the respective homes of the people.

In addition to these two seasons of prayer, the ancient Hebrews prayed at the beginning of the first night watch, while the evening sacrifice was still burning on the altar; as we find recorded of king David in the book of psalms, who prayed morning, noon, and evening. It is also mentioned of Daniel, that he prayed three times a day.

The priests and the Levites were devoted to the service of the temple; but in the service of the various synagogues, persons of any tribe were appointed, if found competent, by the elders who were the rulers of the synagogue.

The synagogues were also used in olden times as courts of justice, more especially in ecclesiastical affairs. The great council of the nation, called the Sanhedrin, whose department was in the temple at Jerusalem, was vested with the power of deciding between life and death. Its authority extended over all the synagogues in Judea, as also over all other places, where the people resided near Jerusalem. The great synagogue consisted of one hundred and twenty elders, among whom were the three later prophets, Hagai, Zacharia, and Malachi. This conclave continued in succession till the days of Simon, the just, the high priest in Jerusalem, who was the last of this school. He was designated the just, because of his devotion and unfeigned piety to his God, and his upright conduct towards his fellow creatures. This conclave were zealously engaged in restoring the holy religion of Israel to its former excellence, which had undergone many corruptions during the captivity and other persecutions which the people endured subsequent to that period. They published correct copies of the bible, and taught the same to the people, in order that they should understand the religion which they professed to follow.

Then it was that the worship of the synagogue consisted of three parts—the reading of the scripture, prayer, and preaching. By the scripture, is understood the pentateuch, portions from the prophets, and Hagiographa.

The pentateuch is divided into fifty-two portions, for the fifty-two weeks in the year; one of these portions is read every Sabbath till the whole pentateuch is finished; in addition to the reading of the law, a chapter from the prophets is read, which dates its origin to the following fact.

In those days, when Antiochus Epiphanes destroyed all the books in the possession of the Jews, he prohibited also the reading of the weekly portions of the law on the Sabbath. The elders then, as a substitute, selected chapters from the prophets, corresponding, in some measure, with the context of the weekly portions of the law. This practice was continued until Judas Maccabees had conquered Antiochus, when the reading of the law was resumed. To commemorate this event, the practice of reading the said portions of the prophets, on Sabbaths and festivals, has been continued among the Jews, and is now in use in all Jewish orthodox synagogues.

Under the head of synagogues, we must notice that the Jews had schools wherein the children were taught to read the law; as, also, academies, in which the rabbins and doctors made comments on the law, and taught the traditions to their pupils. These academies were furnished with many tutors, of whom one was appointed as president, and under whose name the academy was denominated. Of this character, were the two famous schools of Hillel and Shammai, as also the school of the celebrated rabbi, Gamliel, whom we shall have to introduce to the notice of the reader hereafter, when we speak of the compilers of the Mishna and the Talmud. The subject of prayer will form the contents of the next chapter.

CHAPTER X.

Of the origin and introduction of Prayer among the Jews.

The bible informs us that, even in the earliest ages of the world, there existed in the human breast a spontaneous bursting forth of grateful feeling towards God, the benefactor of mankind.

The first specimen we meet with is in the days of Seth, the third son of Adam. "Then began men to call upon the name of the Lord." The same expression is used in the history of the patriarch Abraham, who built altars and prayed to God. His example was followed by Isaac and Jacob, and their immediate descendants. This "calling on the name of the Lord," is what we now understand by the term prayer.

From the several verses in Genesis, which speak of the prayers offered up by the patriarchs, the Talmud infers that the morning prayer was first introduced by Abraham, afternoon prayer by Isaac, and that of the evening by Jacob; and, therefore, it is concluded that prayer was, from the earliest period, held as a regular and stated duty.

After the release of the Israelites from Egyptian bondage, they were initiated into a holy communion by divine revelation on Mount Sinai. The mode of worship then, consisted of regular daily sacrifices, as described in the bible; additional offerings for festivals, or propitiatory, as those offered for sins and transgressions. These last were always accompanied with suitable prayers and confessions.

In this manner, the sinner had to make confession when he brought an offering in expiation of his sins. On the day of atonement, when the high priest presented the offering to the Lord, he had to make confession on behalf of himself and the congregation.

In Deuteronomy, chapter the twenty-sixth, fifth verse, we find a particular form of thanksgiving and confession to be used by the people, when they offered up the first ripe fruits to the Lord in the temple at Jerusalem.

All other addresses to the Almighty appear to have arisen as occasions required. Of this class, we find several instances, such as Moses, Joshua, Hannah, Hezekiah, and others.

Nothing, however, more clearly points out the fact where prayer become an established custom, than the devout and emphatic prayer to the

Almighty by king Solomon, at the dedication of the temple at Jerusalem, which he had raised to the honor and glory of the God of Israel.

The language used by the royal sage on that occasion, so strongly proves the assertion that prayer became an established custom, that we cannot refrain from introducing to the reader the following extract.

"That thine eyes may be open toward this house, night and day, even toward the place of which thou hast said, my name shall be there; that thou mayest hearken unto the prayer which thy servant shall make toward this place. And hearken thou to the supplication of this servant, and of thy people Israel, when they shall pray toward this place; and hear thou in heaven, thy dwelling place, and when thou hearest, forgive."

The royal sage then proceeds to particularize the nature of prayers most likely to be used; as private injuries, national subjugation, want of rain, famine, or pestilence, even the prayer of a stranger not of the people of Israel, &c. Surely, a specimen such as this, must prove an established custom among them to consider it a duty to pray to God for favors conferred, and solicit his protection in the hour of trouble and distress.

The temple at Jerusalem was certainly the consecrated place of regular prayer and sacrifices, for all Israelites who were within its reach; yet, as many lived at too great a distance from this sacred spot, private devotion was no doubt regularly practiced among them. We can trace, in history, many accounts of the existence of places purposely devoted to daily prayer and regular worship. The prophets, of whom we read, at Damascus, Shiloh, Bethel, and Jericho, had, no doubt, a regular form of prayer; for, at Jericho, there was an assemblage called the sons of the prophets.

After the destruction of the first temple, the Jewish nation was driven to Babylon, and from there they became scattered about the neighboring heathen countries. The occasions for prayer and supplication must have increased in such a state of slavery and persecution. Hence their addresses to the Almighty must have become more sincere and more constant. The reflection on their former state in society, compared with that in which they were now placed, must have caused in the people a strong feeling of devotion, leading on to the use of regular and earnest prayer. Then it was, that prayer was the sole solace of the people, while under such persecution.

The prophet Daniel suffered himself to be cast into the lions' den, because he persisted in praying three times a day towards Jerusalem, in defiance of the king's edict, which prohibited any person from worshipping any other God but the idol set up by the king.

In the days of Daniel, it is found that the pure Hebrew used by the Israelites had become much corrupted by the intermixture of the Chaldee and other languages, with which they became conversant by their being so closely united with the strange nations. This caused the holy tongue to be in a great measure forgotten. Nehemiah complains of this, and says: "Their children spake half in the speech of Ashdod, and could not speak in the language of the Jew, but according to the language of the several people."

Ezra, the scribe, who lived in those days, looked on this matter with considerable grief. He was fearful that the people would entirely neglect their holy worship on account of the want of a proper knowledge of the sacred language. And he further saw the consequences would be, that when the people did pray, they would fail to select proper expressions to convey their feelings and sentiments. Ezra, therefore, in conjunction with his conclave, collected, composed, and compiled the prayers in the pure and original Hebrew. They were so arranged as to be suitable for any occasion of private and public devotion, both for the morning and the afternoon, in reference to the regular daily sacrifices offered up in the temple. Also, an additional form of prayer, called "Moosoph" in Hebrew, for those days on which the additional sacrifices had been offered; such as Sabbaths, festivals, and the new moon; also, for the evening sacrifice which burned all night on the altar; likewise, the Nengelah, or concluding prayer of the day of atonement. These are the prayers which have been handed down to the posterity of the Jews throughout the known world.

Ezra and his conclave, who performed this great work, were called "the men of the great assembly or synagogue." The Talmud, Maimonides, and other eminent Jewish authorities, inform us that this synod was composed of one hundred and twenty persons of great piety and learning, among whom were the prophets, Hagai, Zacharia, Malachi, Ezra, Nehemiah, Hananiah, Mishael, and Azaria, together with many other great men, whom we shall notice hereafter.

These prayers were in daily use among the people during the second temple; for in the Mishna, when speaking of the order observed in the daily sacrifices in the temple, it is stated that the prefect who gave the instructions, regularly said to the officiating priests, "repeat ye one blessing," which they did; then the ten commandments, and the shemang. He again said, "repeat ye with the people these blessings," which they did, many of which are in daily use among all orthodox Jews. Besides, as we have before noticed, many Israelites lived at great distances from the temple, and, therefore, it is not reasonable to suppose that God's chosen people should be altogether without some regular formulæ of prayer.

Any person who examines the prayers in daily use among the Israelites, must become sensible of their excellence, and the grateful expressions and high wrought admiration in which they are composed. They are adapted to every situation in life, whether in sorrow or in joy, in grief or in mirth. No one who views the wondrous creation; no one possessed of the slightest spark of gratitude for favors bestowed; nor he who looks forward with hope for relief in the hour of distress, or sickness, can possibly have any language better suited to his feelings, under any circumstances, and on every occasion.

Nothing, perhaps, has tended so much to keep Israel distinct from every other nation in the world, as their religious customs and observances; but more especially so, their language, the sacred original, in which the Lord of hosts manifested himself to his favorite creature; the language in which they pray, and which, in truth, is the only relic of their former glory and paternal heritage. It is the continuance of praying in the Hebrew, which forms, as it were, a communion for their dispersed brethren, from whatever country or clime they may migrate, and constitute themselves into a congregation; a language peculiarly their own—venerable for its antiquity, and sacred from its first promulgation, as being the true channel of divine revelation.

The reader will please understand that our observations, as well as the historical accounts, can only have reference to those prayers and supplications which were composed for the Jew by the men of the great synagogue, as already explained. Alas! that any innovation should have been suffered to mar the beauty of those holy compositions!

There are many more of a sacred character, such as known by the name of "Peyutem," or poetical compositions, which are read in the synagogue on the festivals and other special days. These are of much later date, and have been introduced, from time to time, into the Jewish liturgy, by men eminent for their learning, piety, and devotion. They were written under peculiar circumstances of distress and persecution, during the varied dispersion of the nation, more especially in the eleventh and twelfth centuries.

It was then that the Jews found consolation in the dark storm of persecution, in pouring out their souls in prayer and religious devotion, which they did spontaneously on the different occasions which presented themselves. Their extempore effusions were so characteristic of their pitiful situation, that they made an indelible impression upon the minds, not only of their composers, but also upon those to whom they were recited. To commemorate such events, these compositions were committed to writing. In honor to the authors, the several congregations among whom these pious men lived, introduced them into the festival prayers, and other marked days. These have become embodied in the regular festival and Sabbath prayer book, and have been in constant use among the German and Polish Jews up to the present day. The Portuguese Jews, however, have an entire different formula. Theirs is more ancient than either the German or Polish. It is worth notice, though strange, indeed, that the German Jews, who, in a great measure, omit the recital of these Peyutem, were the very people among whom they were principally composed. It is, however, not our province to discuss here the expediency of such proceedings: we have only to treat of facts; the reader can judge for himself.

Some few exceptions, however, exist. Many of the Peyutem, above mentioned, claim a much earlier date, and are from the pen of some of the most holy men of the ancient race of Israel. These compositions will be found in the additional service of new year and day of atonement; also, those prayers called propitiatory—as the *Selechous*, recited previously to and during the penitential days. They have in all ages been admired for their beauty of diction, and sublimity of language, and are highly calculated to inspire the reader with profound awe and veneration, when addressing them to his creator.

It remains now only for the Hebrew language to become a primary object of study among all classes, so that they may learn to appreciate the beauty of God's own language, and thus to be prepared with devotion whenever engaged in prayer, either in private or in public. If such were the case, those who labor in the good cause would be fully repaid, when, by their exertions, they should succeed in awakening the dormant feelings of the negligent to such a duty of prayer as may be acceptable to the creator of mankind. Then will the intelligent mind become sensible of the excellence of the ancient and holy liturgy of the chosen people of God.

CHAPTER XI.

Of the Ureem and Thumeem.

"And thou shalt put in the breast-plate of judgment the Ureem and Thumeem." Exodus, 28, 30. What the Ureem and Thumeem were is not distinctly explained in the bible.

That they were not the twelve precious stones contained in the breast-plate, as some have erroneously imagined, is quite clear; for we do not find that God directed Moses to make the Ureem and Thumeem, as he did when he said, "And thou shalt make the breast-plate," &c., &c.

It is plain from the text itself, that they were something in addition to the breast-plate, and put therein, after it was finished, by Moses himself; and therefore God says, "And thou shalt put into the breast-plate of judgment the Ureem and Thumeem."

From this fact, it is evident that there was something additional placed in the breast-plate by Moses; and for this reason, it is supposed that it was made double, that it might the more conveniently hold them. It now remains to inquire what the Ureem and Thumeem in reality were, and what the particular use of them. As to the former, there are various opinions among the learned. Many celebrated Christian divines have ventured many erroneous definitions on the subject. According to the opinions of the most erudite and pious Hebrew doctors and rabbins, the following appears to be the most reasonable view of the case.

It was, say the rabbins, the Tetragrammaton, or ineffable name of the Deity, which Moses was commanded to place in the breast-plate, and was consecrated to holy purposes. It was vested with divine power to give an oracular reply from God to any counsel being asked of him by the high priest, during the time in which he wore it. Now, as the answer came immediately from God, it was therefore properly designated "asking counsel of God." As to the Ureem and Thumeem, it was especially to ask counsel of God on such momentous occasions only, in relation to the Jewish nation.

In the Mishna of *Yoomah* are explained three express conditions necessary to be observed in the asking of counsel by the Ureem and Thumeem.

FIRST.—Concerning the person inquiring. He must not be a private person. He must be either the king, the president of the Sanhedrin, who presided over the whole nation, the general of the army, or some other noble prince, or governor in Israel.

SECOND.—Concerning the nature of the question. It must not be respecting the affairs of private persons; but such only as relate to the public interest of the whole nation, either of church or state.

THIRD.—Concerning the person who presents the question. He must be the high priest, clothed in his pontifical robes, and his breast-plate with the Ureem and Thumeem.

The learned Maimonides observes in his celebrated work, "Moreh Nevoocheem," or a "*guide to the perplexed*," part second, chapter forty-five, that the Ureem and Thumeem was a degree of the divine inspiration. Speaking of the different degrees or orders of prophecy, he says: "And thus every high priest who inquired by the Ureem and Thumeem was of this order, as already mentioned."

The divine presence rested on him, and he spoke by the holy spirit, that is, he delivered his answers with the assistance of the holy inspiration. According to this opinion, it was but one degree below the spirit of prophecy. All the learned and eminent men among the Jews say, that the manner of asking counsel, and receiving the answer thereto, was as follows.

The person who inquired did not make the request in an audible tone; but in such a way as one who is at his devotion pronounces the words, sufficiently loud to be heard by none but himself.

The question being made, the priest looked into the breast-plate, and on perceiving some letters on the stone of the same glistening, he, by combining them together, obtained the answer. We shall best exemplify the foregoing by the following passage from the book of Judges.

"Now, after the death of Joshua, it came to pass that the children of Israel asked the Lord, saying, who shall go up for us against the Canaanites first, to fight against them." The reply was: "*Yehuda Yangaleh*" or "Judah shall go up;" for as soon as the question was propounded, the priest looked into the breast-plate, and seeing the name of Judah appear prominent, he was assured that Judah was the tribe. The priest looked again, and beheld the *Yod* shine, the *Ngain* from the name of *Simeon*; then the Lamed from another name, and the *Heh* from another; these four letters being put together made the word "*Yangaleh*" which signifies, "*He shall go up.*" When the priest found that no more letters glistened, he knew immediately that the answer was completed. Hence the reason why they are called *Ureem*, which signifies *Light*, from the shining of the letters; and *Thumeem*, or perfection, as the answer was thus complete and perfected.

This fact distinguished the Jewish oracles from the pretended heathen oracles, which were always delivered in an enigmatical and ambiguous manner. The Jewish oracles were always clear and explicit, never falling short of perfection, either in the manifestation or the certainty of the truth thereof.

During the existence of the second temple, the Ureem and Thumeem were not consulted; for when the ark and coverlid, the cherubim and the two tables of stone, disappeared at the destruction of the first temple, the breast-plate with the *Ureem* and *Thumeem* shared the same fate. Notwithstanding that on the return of the Jews to Jerusalem, they had the pontifical robes, with the breast-plate with four rows of stones, engraved with the names of the tribes of Israel; yet no question was ever asked, and consequently no communication ever received from the *Ureem* and *Thumeem*. Two reasons are assigned for this.

FIRST.—Because the said *Ureem* and *Thumeem* were instituted to ask counsel of the Lord of such things which concerned *all* the tribes of Israel, and the common interest of the whole nation. Now, there being at that time the tribes of Judah and Benjamin only, these oracles could not *be* consulted, the common interest of the nation having then ceased.

SECONDLY—And possibly the principal reason, was, that the *Tetragrammaton*, or ineffable name of the Deity, which Moses put between the folds of the breast-plate, was wanting. This being the most important part, and the very essence of the whole—when the cause ceased, the effect also ceased.

CHAPTER XII.

Of the Mishna, or Oral Law.

The Pentateuch, or written law, was communicated by God to Moses, and by him to the people of Israel at different times, and adapted to the various seasons, places and circumstances during the forty years' sojournment in the wilderness.

The mode adopted in instructing the Israelites in the wilderness in the divine law was as follows: Every passage or chapter of the written law, whether historical or preceptive, was written by Moses, as received from God himself, which he placed before his council or senate, called, afterwards, Sanhedrin, as well as before the whole body of the people. This council consisted of seventy elders, or senators, the most learned and pious among the nation, of whom Moses was the president. Every chapter of the law was explained by Moses according to the oral tradition, which he received coeval with the written law. The agreement of these two was proved in such a way as to show that the oral law is the true and genuine spirit and sense of the Pentateuch; that they are so intimately and inseparably connected with each other as to be considered as one and indivisible.

Aaron, the high priest, was honored with the appointment of repeating, for the instruction of the people, all the learning taught by his brother Moses. Aaron was succeeded by his sons. Then came the elders who gathered together all the Israelites and placed them in their several academies for the study of the law. Every individual of Israel was permitted to make memoranda of the oral law, in order to assist the memory, for personal and private convenience, but the public instruction was taught orally. This oral tradition was transmitted from Moses down to the days of the celebrated Rabbi, Judah the Prince, son of the learned Simon the Just, about a hundred and fifty years after the destruction of the second temple. After the death of Moses, Joshua the son of Nun, his successor, taught the said law in his Sanhedrin, and delivered it to the elders who succeeded him; and in like manner the tradition of the Mishna was successively transferred from generation to generation, and was concluded by Rabbi Judah, above named, who flourished in the reign of the Emperor Antoninus, by whom he was honored with the title of Prince, and invested with a supremacy of power for his office. It was generally believed in those days that there never rose up in Israel any man like unto him, in whom so much piety, wealth and glory were united.

It was in consequence of his extreme piety and devotion to spiritual purposes only, and divesting himself of all worldly cares and pleasures, that he was designated Rabbinu Hakodesh, or the Holy Rabbi. This pious man, acting as president of the Sanhedrin, consulted his colleagues, who, perceiving the decline of literature, such as contained in the oral law at that period, and fearful of the consequences thereof to the nation at large, took into their serious consideration the necessity of adopting some plan by which such tradition should not be entirely forgotten. They saw and felt that the many sufferings and persecutions inflicted upon their co-religionists would ultimately be the cause of the loss of that knowledge which was so dear to them as God's own people. That it would be impossible for future generations to understand the practical part of the divine precepts as embodied in the Pentateuch. It was therefore with holy zeal that they judged it proper to collect and compile all the oral tradition explanatory of the written law and commit the same to writing, in order that it should be handed down to posterity. This is the same Mishna now in existence among the Jews at this day. It is written in short sentences and aphorisms, and generally considered to be in pure Hebrew, with some few exceptions. It contains full elucidations of the Pentateuch, as admitted by the most eminent Jewish doctors of all ages, who testify that without such elucidations the written law would have remained a sealed book to the world at large.

In the following chapter we shall treat of the Gemara, or Completion, usually called the Talmud, the same being a commentary on the Mishna.

For the present, we shall content ourselves by laying before our readers a succinct account of the contents of the Mishna.

The Mishna is divided into six general heads, called in Hebrew, Sedoreem, orders or classes. The first is styled Zeroeëm, which signifies *seeds*, and is subdivided into eleven sections.

FIRST—BEROCHOUT, OR BLESSINGS.—This section treats of the laws directing the order of prayers and thanksgivings for the produce of the earth, and for all other benefits conferred on man by the beneficent creator; with the consideration as to time and place when they are to be said or repeated.

SECOND—PYOH, OR CORNER.—This section treats of those laws which direct the leaving of the corner of the field, as the portion for the benefit of the poor, as commanded in the book of Leviticus.

THIRD—DEMAI, OR DOUBTFUL.—This treats of such things of which there exists some doubt, as to tithes having been paid for them, the Israelites not being allowed to eat of anything until it had been tithed.

FOURTH—TERUMOUS, OR OBLATIONS.—This section points out such things of which a portion was to be set apart as devoted to the use of the priests.

FIFTH—SHEVINGIS, OR SEVENTH.—This section explains the laws of the seventh year, called the Sabbatical year, during which period the land was to remain at rest, and lie fallow; and during which time all debts were remitted and obligations canceled.

SIXTH—KILLAYIM, OR MIXTURES.—This portion lays down the laws which prohibit the mixing or joining of things together of an opposite or different nature or species; as, the sowing of various kinds of seeds in one and the same spot of ground; or suffering cattle of different kinds to engender; or the grafting a scion of one species of plant on the sk of another of a different character.

SEVENTH—MANGSIRE REESHOUN, OR FIRST TITHE. This section signifies the first tithes, and treats of the laws of the said tithes which shall be apportioned to the Levites.

EIGHTH—MANGSIRE SHYNEE, OR SECOND TITHES. This treats of the laws of the second tithes, which were to be taken up to Jerusalem, and there to be eaten, or to be redeemed, and the produce expended at Jerusalem in peace offerings.

FIFTH—CHALAH, LOAF, OR CAKE.—This section speaks of the laws relative to setting apart a cake of dough for the priests; of the description of dough the cake should be, and what kind of dough was prohibited from being used for the purpose.

TENTH—ORLAH, OR UNCIRCUMCISED.—This section explains the law touching the illegality of eating the fruit of any tree until the fifth year of its growth. As follows: During the first three years of its bearing fruit, it must not be eaten; the fourth year it was holy to the Lord; and on the fifth year, it was permitted to be eaten by the owner thereof.

ELEVENTH—BICKUREEM, OR FIRST RIPE FRUITS. This section treats of the manner in which the first ripe fruits were to be offered up in the holy temple at Jerusalem.

The second general head or class is called *Seder Moed*, or order of festivals. It is so denominated because it treats of all those laws which were made concerning festivals and days of solemn observance. This second class is divided into twelve sections.

FIRST—SABBATH, OR REST.—This is so called because it treats of all the laws respecting the Sabbath. This division contains twenty-four chapters.

SECOND—EYRUVEEN, OR MIXTURES, OR ASSOCIATIONS.—This section shows in what manner food might be conveyed from house to house on the Sabbath day. All the inhabitants of the court or place in which the association was formed, were allowed so to do. It also explains the rules laid down for any journey to be made on the Sabbath.

THIRD—PESOCHIM, OR PASSOVER.—This portion treats of all the laws, customs, and ceremonies, to be observed at the offering up of the paschal lamb on the eve of the festival of Passover.

FOURTH—SHEKOLEEM, OR SHEKELS.—This treats of the half shekels, which every Israelite, whether rich or poor, was bound to pay every year towards defraying the expenses of the daily sacrifices offered up on the altar in Jerusalem.

FIFTH—YOUMOH, OR DAY.—This section treats of the great and solemn day of atonement; pointing out the ceremonies of the day, and the duties of the high priest on that holy occasion. It also speaks of the sacrifices which were to be offered up as expiations for the sins of the people.

SIXTH—SUCCOH, OR TABERNACLE.—This portion treats of the feast of tabernacles. It points out in what manner the tabernacle should be built; the use of the palm tree, the citron, the myrtle, and the willow of the brook, which were ordered to be taken and used on the said festival.

SEVENTH—YOUM TOUV, OR FESTIVAL.—It is called, also, Bytsoh, or Egg, being the word with which it commences. This section contains the laws and regulations for the due observance of the festivals of the Lord. It points out what work may, or may not, be lawfully done on any of the festivals which are called holy days of convocation, on which all manual labor or traffic is prohibited.

EIGHTH—ROUSH HASHONO, OR NEW YEAR.—This treats of the laws and solemnities of the sacred day of the new year; such as the sounding of the *shouphar* or *cornet*; of the prayers and regular service of that holy occasion. It describes, also, the ceremony for the observance at the appearance of the new moon, by which all the holy days were regulated by the Sanhedrin during the existence of the second temple.

NINTH—TANGANEES, OR FAST.—This division treats of the different fasts held throughout the year, and the manner in which they are to be observed by every Israelite. These fasts are held on different occasions for various reasons, and purposes; such as days of repentance, humiliation, and of calamity and misfortune which befel the nation in the several ages of persecution.

TENTH—MEGILLOH, OR ROLL OF THE BOOK OF ESTHER.—This section treats of the feast of Purim, and directs how the roll shall be written and read on this festival. It speaks of many other rules and regulations to be observed on this feast, which commemorates the miraculous deliverance of the Jewish people from the hands of the wicked Haman, who contemplated the destruction of the whole nation. It also treats of the laws concerning the synagogue, and the reading of the holy law on the several days of solemn and religious observance throughout the year.

ELEVENTH—MOED KOTON, OR LESSER FESTIVALS. This treats of such work as may or may not be done during the middle days of the passover and tabernacle holidays. It is, therefore, called Moed Koton, as the middle days of the said festivals are considered less holy than the first and last two days. It contains, also, the laws regulating the conduct of mourners.

TWELFTH—HAGIGAH, OR FESTIVAL OFFERINGS. This section specifies the laws relating to the offerings made on the different festivals; the description of the persons; how they are to be qualified, and in what manner they are to appear before the Lord on the three great festivals in every year, when all the Israelites that possibly could, were expected to be in attendance at the holy city of Jerusalem.

The third general head, or class, is called Nosheem, or women. This is subdivided into seven sections.

FIRST—YEVOMOUS, OR MARRIAGE.—This section is so called, as it treats of the laws by which one brother is expected to marry the relict of his deceased brother. It shows how, and when, the obligation shall take place; the duties and the ceremonies to be observed at the performance of the same.

SECOND—KESUVOUS, OR DOCUMENTS.—This speaks of the laws relating to marriage contracts, and dowries, and of estates, whether real or personal, which may fall to some married women; how the same shall be disposed of, by, or allotted to, the said party or parties.

THIRD—NEDOREEM, OR VOWS.—This treats of such vows which, when made, become binding, and by what persons such vows shall be made; how vows are considered null and void, since the husband has the power of confirming or annulling the vows of his wife. This law is very particularly specified, as to how such may be done; and the class of vows which fall under the control of the husband, and those which do not.

FOURTH—NOZEER, OR NAZARITE.—This section treats of those laws which guide the different classes of Nazarites who take upon themselves the vows of abstinence.

FIFTH—SOTAH, OR TO TURN ASIDE.—This treats of the enactments relating to trials occasioned through jealousy between man and wife; the nature of the punishment inflicted on the woman, if it be proved that she had been guilty of the crime of adultery.

SIXTH—GITTEN, OR LETTER OF DIVORCE.—This treats of the laws of divorce. It explains when, and under what circumstances, a divorce may be granted. It directs also all the formulæ to be used and observed in all cases of divorce.

SEVENTH—KEDUSHEEN, OR BETROTHING.—This treats of the laws, customs, and ceremony of betrothing; the forms, rites, and regulations to be observed at the solemnization of the marriage according to the laws of Moses and Israel.

The fourth general head, or class, is called Nezeekeen, or Damages. This class is divided into eight sections; the first of which is again subdivided into three separate sections, as follow.

FIRST—BOVOH KAMMA, OR FIRST GATE.—This first section treats of all such damages, which may be recovered for injuries done, either by man or beast.

SECOND—BOVOH MEZIAH, OR MIDDLE GATE.—This treats of the laws of usury. It explains what is, and what is not, considered an act of usury. It speaks also on matters of special trust; of letting or hire, and such like transactions between man and man.

THIRD—BOVOH BOSROH, OR LAST GATE.—This treats of the laws relating to commerce, copartnership, buying and selling; also, the laws of inheritance, and the right of succession.

The above three sections are called by the Talmud and Mishna, gates, because, in the East, the courts of law were held within the gates of the city.

SECOND—SANHEDREEN, OR SENATE.—This speaks of the great senate, as also of the minor courts of judicature; of the causes for trial, and the nature of the punishment inflicted for the several crimes; the four kinds of death, as the penalty for capital offenses. It describes, also, very minutely, the mode to be adopted by the Judges in the examination of witnesses.

THIRD—MACCOUS, OR PUNISHMENT.—This portion treats more especially of that which may constitute false testimony, or inadmissible evidence; the laws relative to the forty stripes inflicted on the delinquent; the reason why the rabbins directed that only thirty-nine stripes should be inflicted instead of forty, as stated in the bible; also, the manner in which the said punishment should be administered. It relates, likewise, the regulations to be observed by such persons who were compelled to seek shelter in the cities of refuge.

Fourth—Shevungous, or Oaths.—This section explains the laws to be observed in the administration of an oath; in what cases an oath shall or shall not be submitted to the contending parties; who shall or who shall not be considered qualified to take the oath.

Fifth—Adoyous, Testimonies or Evidences. This treats of the decisions of the many important cases, collected from the evidence and testimony of the most eminent and learned rabbins and doctors of the great Sanhedrin of olden times.

Sixth—Avoudoh Zoroh, or Idolatry.—This section is so called, as it treats of all manner of idolatry. It is also entitled the "*the worship of the planets.*" It explains the manner and form of the different modes of worship, as practised by the idolatrous nations, with the view of preventing the Israelite from becoming contaminated by them.

Seventh—Ovous, or Fathers.—This section contains the history of those holy fathers who, in their respective ages, successively received by tradition the oral law; from the days of Moses, the great lawgiver, down to the period when it was compiled and committed to writing by the celebrated rabbinu Hakodesh. It contains, also, many of the wise sayings, aphorisms, and moral maxims of the learned men, and is therefore called the "Ethics of the fathers."

Eighth—Houroyous, or Precepts.—This section is so called, because it treats of the punishment and penalty to be inflicted on those who should presumptuously act against, or teach anything in opposition to, the decrees and decisions of the great Sanhedrin at Jerusalem.

The fifth general head, or class, is called Kodosheem, or holy things. It is subdivided into eleven sections.

First—Zevocheem, or Sacrifices.—This section treats of the order to be observed in offering up the cattle for sacrifices, and points out their nature and quality. It also relates the time and the place; and specifies by whom they were to be killed and brought up as an offering upon the altar of the Lord.

Second—Minochous, or Meat Offerings.—This portion treats of the oblations of oil, flour, and wine, proper for each offering; and of the two waive loaves, which were to be made of fine flour, such as were offered up, on the festival of pentecost.

Third—Choolin, or Profane.—This section points out that which is clean, and that which is unclean; what may and what may not be lawfully eaten; and the law which prohibits the killing of the dam and its young, both in one day. It also shows the law prohibiting the eating of the "sinew which shrank;" and the law forbidding the taking of the dam with its young. It, moreover, embraces the laws appertaining to the killing of cattle and fowl for domestic use; and who may, and who may not, be permitted to kill the animals for food to be eaten by Israelites.

FOURTH—BECHOUROUS, OR FIRST BORN.—This section treats of the laws relating to the first born of both man and cattle; pointing out in what manner, and at which period, they were to be redeemed, either with money, or brought up as an offering to the Lord. It speaks also of the tithes of all manner of cattle.

FIFTH—EYRACHIN, OR VALUATION, OR ESTIMATION.—This section treats of the manner in which things devoted to the Almighty are valued, so that they may be redeemed and applied to ordinary purposes; as also how the priest shall value a field, devoted or sacrificed to the Lord by its owner.

SIXTH—TEMUROH, OR EXCHANGE.—This portion explains how far it may be lawful to exchange one sacred thing for another; as, whether an animal which had been consecrated as an offering to be sacrificed to the Lord might be exchanged. In most cases, where an animal had been consecrated to the Lord, and then exchanged, both the animal and its substitute became sacred.

SEVENTH—KERISUS, OR EXCISIONS.—This section relates to offenses which, if wantonly committed, were punished by the offender being cut off from among the people, called *Kohrice*. It points out, at the same time, what offenders were liable to this punishment. It likewise explains how those who had offended through accident, had to bring a sin or trespass offering.

EIGHTH—MENGELOH, OR TRESPASS.—This portion treats of the nature of the trespass made by converting such things which have been consecrated and devoted to holy purposes, to profane or unholy matters.

NINTH—TOMEED, OR CONTINUAL OFFERINGS.—Herein are specified the daily sacrifices, and the description as to how, and in what manner, they were to be offered upon the altar of the Lord.

TENTH—MIDDOUS, OR DIMENSIONS.—This book is so called, because it speaks of the dimensions and proportions of the temple. It describes the mount on which the temple stood, and the full extent of the outer court. This was considered requisite to be known; for whoever had become unclean, from any circumstance whatever, was prohibited from entering the temple on pain of excision.

ELEVENTH—KONEEM, OR NESTS.—This section speaks of the birds, such as pigeons or turtle-doves, which were brought as offerings by the poor, instead of the more expensive, which they were unable to bring. The smaller value was equally acceptable to the God of mercy and kindness.

The sixth general head, or class, is entitled Taharous, or purifications. It is divided into twelve sections.

FIRST—KYLEEM, OR VESSELS, UTENSILS.—This book is so called, because it treats of the pollutions incident to vessels, and how they are to be purified from such uncleanness. It treats also of the manner in which garments of every description may be purified, in the event of their becoming polluted or defiled by uncleanness of any kind.

SECOND—OHOLOUS, OR TENTS.—This section treats of the manner in which houses become polluted; the nature of such pollutions; and how far those who enter such dwellings may thereby become contaminated, and how they may be purified.

THIRD—NEGOIM, OR PLAGUES, OR DISEASES.—This book explains all the laws relative to the plague of leprosy; whether on man or beast, dwellings or garments. It shows how and in what manner infection took place; and how the things or persons so afflicted may become purified.

FOURTH—POROH, OR HEIFER.—This section speaks of the laws relating to the red heifer; how the said heifer should be burned to ashes, in order to make the water for purification; and in what manner all defilements, contracted by the touch or contact of a dead body, could be purified by means of the ashes of the red heifer.

FIFTH—TAHAROUS, OR PURIFICATIONS.—This portion treats of all those laws pertaining to such defilements which may be contracted otherwise than by the touch of a dead body; and of the manner purification may, and can take place.

SIXTH—MIKVOOUS, OR BATHS.—This section treats of the laws and regulations for baths to be used for purification by ablutions; of all persons who may have from any cause whatever become unclean. Herein is also specified the manner in which the bath should be constructed, and the quantity of water required for every ablution.

SEVENTH—NIDDOH, OR SEPARATION.—This portion explains all the laws relating to the pollutions and purifications of women after child-birth, and on every occasion of uncleanness.

EIGHTH—MACHSHEREEN.—This section explains in what manner seed or fruit became susceptible of defilement or pollution through the admixture of liquids.

NINTH—ZOBEEM, OR ISSUES.—This portion treats of the laws relating to the impurities arising from the issues of the body; and points out how and when they are deemed unclean; and how and in what manner either persons or things may become affected by their pollution.

TENTH—TIBBUL YOUM, OR PURIFICATION OF A DAY.—This portion speaks of persons who may become unclean, and require ablution to purify them; which purification cannot be considered complete until the setting of the sun on the same day when the purification shall take place.

ELEVENTH—YODOYEEM, OR HANDS.—This section treats of the laws and regulations for cleansing the hands from any uncleanness; and the custom and ceremony to be observed in washing the hands on the different occasions.

TWELFTH—UKTSEEM, OR STALKS.—This last section is so called, because it explains how the touching of the stalks of any sort of fruit may convey pollution to the fruit itself.

SYNOPSIS OF THE FOREGOING MISHNA.

No. 1.—Seder Zeroeem contains	11 sections.
No. 2.—Seder Moed contains	12 sections.
No. 3.—Seder Nosheem contains	7 sections.
No. 4.—Seder Nezekeen contains	10 sections.
No. 5.—Seder Kodosheem contains	11 sections.
No. 6.—Seder Taharous contains	12 sections.
Total	63 sections.

CHAPTER XIII.

Of the Gemara, or Completion, which is usually styled Talmud.

In the foregoing chapter we described the manner in which the Mishna was compiled, together with its contents, from its first delivery by Moses till the time of its being committed to writing by Rabbi Judah the Prince. We shall now proceed in regular order to explain what the Talmud is, and how it was composed by the several learned men among the Jews both in Jerusalem and in Babylon.

The compilation of the Talmud ranks among the most ancient Hebrew writings. It consists of two distinct heads—the Mishna and the Gemara, and both together form the Talmud.

The Mishna, as already explained, chiefly contains the oral or traditional laws transmitted down to posterity from the time of Moses the Lawgiver, to that of Rabbi Judah the Prince or Nassi.

The Gemara consists of expositions and comments on the Mishna, as also various other subjects connected with Jewish literature, and more especially Jewish theology. It contains also treatises on moral philosophy, ethics, mathematics, astronomy and chronology, and many other branches of the different sciences known in those days. The Gemara or expositions on the Mishna was commenced in the days of the Rabbins, Gamaliel and Simeon, the two sons of Rabbi Judah the Holy, about the year 3980 of the creation, and was completed and compiled into one body by Rav Ashi, President, and Raviny, Vice President, who are considered the actual compilers of the Babylonian Talmud. This took place about the year 4260.

The authors of the Talmud in general are styled Amooroim, dictators, as they dictated the several explications of the Mishna, as discussed in the different schools, and which are all found in the Talmud. The comments and expositions are known by the name of Gemara, which signifies completion, because therein is fully explained all the traditional doctrines of the Jewish law and its religion. The Mishna is the text, the Gemara the comment, or glossary, and both together form the Talmud.

There are two Talmudim. The first is styled Talmud Yerushalmi, or Jerusalem Talmud. This was compiled by Rabbi Jochanan in five sedorim or divisions. This Talmud does not contain the whole of the Mishna. It was completed about the year 4060. The second Talmud is called Talmud Bably, or Babylonian Talmud, which was completed about two hundred years after the other Talmud. The Talmud Yerushalmi is the least esteemed of the two, and consequently less studied and quoted by the learned among Israel. It is the Babylonian Talmud which is usually studied and consulted in all points of jurisprudence, as connected with all religious affairs, both in, and out, of the synagogue. It is therefore to be understood, that whenever the Talmud is simply notified, it means the Babylonian Talmud; as the other Talmud is never quoted, unless particularly and expressly mentioned.

The Talmud Bably is arranged in the following order. The Mishna forms the text, and the Gemara is annexed as the comment or glossary. The same order is observed as with the Mishna, although it must be observed that the Gemara appears only on thirty-six sections, whereas the whole of the Mishna contains sixty-three sections, as explained in the foregoing chapter. The order of the Talmud is as follows:

No. 1.—Seder Zeroeem contains	1 section.
No. 2.—Seder Moed contains	11 sections.
No. 3.—Seder Nosheem contains	7 sections.
No. 4.—Seder Nezekeen contains	8 sections.
No. 5.—Seder Kodosheem contains	8 sections.
No. 6.—Seder Taharous contains	1 section.
Total	36 sections.

CHAPTER XIV.

APPENDIX.

Having given a brief description of the Mishna and the Talmud, and their contents, we now direct the attention of the reader to the following observations, as a summary to the preceding two chapters.

The Pentateuch, or Five Books of Moses, is generally understood by the term "written law," and the Talmud as the oral or traditional law. The oral law was handed down from Moses to Joshua, from the elders to the prophets, and from them to the Great Synod, which consisted of one hundred and twenty of the most learned men of the age, and in like manner from time to time, until the days of Rabbi Judah, already mentioned. This great man, seriously contemplating the state of his nation as regarded their religious affairs, and perceiving that those who were learned in the law were gradually diminishing in number, feared that the knowledge of the oral law might ultimately be forgotten, and with it the essential portion of the law of Moses. In the true spirit of devotion and piety, this Rabbi collected all the doctrines and precepts which had been taught orally, down to that period, and with the assistance of his pious colleagues, committed them to writing, and arranged them in the order of the Mishna, as already described. After the Mishna had been written, and presented to the nation at large, it was received by them with a general and unanimous consent. It was universally approved, and was held by them as an authentic document, delivered to Moses by the Almighty, while on the mount, as an explanation of the written law. The prevailing opinion among the people then was, that the Mishna had been handed down by tradition, and they were confirmed in such opinion by the conviction that the same had been taught to them in their youth in the various schools and academies which were established for such purposes. It was then considered expedient by the learned in those days, that some further explanation should be given, in order to render the Mishna more intelligible to the general class of readers.

With this view, some of the most eminent among the Jewish doctors, taught in the schools the oral law together with the signification thereof, and in this way they illustrated all the most abstruse and difficult passages by useful and instructive commentaries. These illustrations and glossaries increased from time to time, which formed the Talmud, such as it is at present in the possession of the Israelites. It abounds with aphorisms and ethics, which were introduced by the Rabbins and Doctors who composed the Talmud, in the course of their discussions. It was in this manner, that they supported the opinions advanced by them on the various subjects upon which they treated. These subjects were frequently illustrated by moral tales and allegories, such being the tutelar system prevalent among most of the oriental nations in those days.

In the said Talmud the Rabbins taught also the various arts and sciences, such as known in those times, although it may be conceded that they may not have reached to such perfection as in the present enlightened age; nevertheless the principle was known by the Israelites of old, and practically applied by them as far as necessity demanded. It is well known that astronomy, geometry, architecture, physics, natural philosophy, as well as many of the other sciences, were in high cultivation both before and after the Babylonian captivity.

The building of the tabernacle in the wilderness—the beautiful temple of Solomon,—the superb edifice erected by Herod the Great, may certainly be advanced as specimens of the science of architecture, in which must naturally be included that of geometry. It cannot be denied that the Jews were also famous in hydraulics, aqueducts, etc., military tactics and war implements, engineering, agriculture, etc.

That astronomy was successfully cultivated by the Israelites of old, is proved by the perpetual chronological calendar which was formed and brought to perfection in the days of the Talmudical doctors. This calendar is composed both of the lunar and solar revolutions. Though it may not be strictly the province of this chapter to treat upon this subject, the reader will excuse the digression, in order to introduce a short extract of this calculation to show the basis upon which the same is founded, and prove that a knowledge of astronomy existed in those days, by the teachers of the Talmud. According to the Mosaic Law, the Israelites are directed to calculate the year and compute their holy days according to the lunar year. Twelve lunar, *synodical revolutions, i.e.* 29 days, 12 hours, 44 minutes and 3 seconds, compose one simple year. Thus we make sometimes 353, 354, 355 days, allowing for fractions. Yet the *Epactem* of 10 days, 21 hours, 11 minutes and 20 seconds, in which the solar year exceeds the lunar, might be the cause, that the holy days would be removed from their respective seasons,—which would be the case, when calculating by the lunar only. So that in a period of seventeen years the feast of Passover would be in the autumn instead of the spring, and the feast of tabernacle in spring instead of the autumn. On this account it was that the Jewish chronologists took care to remedy this defect, by forming alternately, sometimes to compose the year of thirteen lunar months, as 383, 384, 385 days, for which reason they adopted a period of 19 years, in which they formed seven complete years,—as the 3, 6, 8, 11, 14, 17, 19, complete of thirteen lunar months, and the interval twelve years, *simple*, of twelve lunar months only; and in this periodical calculation of 19 years, according to the above rotation of twelve *simple* and seven *complete* years, the *lunar* and *solar* years then agree, without any variation whatever.[A] Hence it is that the Jewish calculation is very exactly and astronomically contrived, for it has never failed since its first introduction, now nearly fifteen centuries. This is a sufficient proof that the science of astronomy was known to the ancient Israelites.

We have already stated, that the Talmud contains many allegories, aphorisms, ethics, etc., which, it must be observed, are not to be interpreted in their literal sense, but as being intended to convey some moral and instructive lesson,—such being the system peculiar to oriental nations. This system not having been clearly understood by many of the Jews and Gentiles in both ancient and modern times, has led to the belief that the whole of the Talmud, as it now exists, is of divine origin. Now in justice to the authors of the Talmud, it must be stated, that they never intended to convey any such idea; their object was simply to render their discussions and dissertations intelligible to their coreligionists of those days, and that it should be carefully handed down to posterity. With this view it was, that the compilers of the Talmud left the work in its original and genuine state, with all the arguments and disputations as given by the authors in the various ages, so that they might not be charged with having interpolated it with ideas of their own, foreign to the views and intentions of the original authors of the work. This is sufficient to show that the *whole* of the Talmud never was considered by the learned, as having a divine origin; but *those* portions of the Mishna, illustrative of the written law, as already explained, were received as divine, having been successively transmitted by oral tradition, from Moses to Rabbi Judah, the Prince, and by him placed before the world and handed down unalloyed to succeeding generations. In coming ages, the learned among Israel, desirous that the study of the Talmud should not be entirely lost, have added comments and glossaries, in order to render the work as easy as possible to the comprehension of the student. The Talmud contains, not, as has been said, the narrow-minded sentiments of bigots, but the devout and conscientious discussions of men deeply impressed with the love of divine providence, and anxious to inculcate that love in others by precept and observation.

It was wisely remarked by the celebrated Luzzato, "that the ancient Rabbies were the incorrupt reporters of the ceremonials and rites of the Jews, and *no innovators!* that they did not attempt to grasp a subject they could not comprehend, nor seek to hide by sophistical arguments, eloquently clothed, a truth that was apparent." *No!* for, says the Venetian sage, they spoke of things to the study of which their whole lives had been devoted, and their piety gave weight to their opinions.

We are aware, however, that we are open to severe criticisms; but we trust that our remarks may neither shock the ear of the more enlightened portion of the Jewish nation, nor incur the displeasure of those, who still believe it to be a crime to urge a word respecting this time honored production. Much has been said on this subject. Whilst some have labored incessantly to enforce the divinity of the Talmud—others again, either from prejudice or other unholy motives, have set at nought the entire composition, and condemned it as useless in the present age. How far the latter may be justified in the promulgation of such sentiments, may be easily ascertained by a glance at Judaism at the present, in view of the strife and contention between the Orthodox and the Reform, with but little benefit to Judaism in general. The reader will look "on this picture and on that" and decide for himself.

We might quote many authorities of high standing among the Jewish literati, such as existed formerly in the schools of Jamnia, Tiberias, Surah, Pombeditha, etc.; and in subsequent ages, those unrivalled Luminaries that appeared in Spain and France, Germany and Poland, who have recommended the study of the Talmud as a guide to the perfect understanding of the holy writings. On the present occasion we prefer citing that which has been said of its merits by other divines, differing from the Jew in faith.

A celebrated Christian divine of the Catholic church who flourished in the fourth century, Aurelio Augustino, in a work called "The City of God," makes the following remarks:

"For, indeed, that nation, that people, that state, that republic, the Israelites, to whom was given the eloquence of God, in no way confounded the pseudo-prophets with their true prophets. But by a unanimous consent, and differing in nothing among themselves, they recognized the latter as the depositaries of the sacred writings, and considered them the authors. These true prophets were philosophers, that is, lovers of wisdom: being themselves wise men, they were theologians, prophets, and teachers of probity and piety. Whoever therefore lives and grows wise according to their doctrines, lives and grows wise not according to the doctrines of men, but according to the *doctrines of God*, who spoke through them."

"He further states, that as the love of virtue, with which these philosophers were deeply imbued, is the foundation of true belief, and the basis of all religion, so their works, coming from so pure, so enlightened, and so pious a source, are entitled to be received, not only by Jews, but by men of all creeds, as guides to the true knowledge of God and to that state of spiritual bliss, which it should be our sole aim in this life to attain," for which reason, in his first book, "*De Arcanis Catholicæ Veritatis*," he strongly urged the propriety of having the Talmud translated into Latin, that it might be studied in the schools of Italy.

Peter Galatino, a learned Franciscan monk, who flourished in the early part of the sixteenth century, was known to be a great persecutor of the Jews. Yet in speaking of the sacred writings and Jewish literature in general, he expressed himself nearly in the following terms: That he regarded the Talmud as a divine work, and that he considered every part of it as perfect, and adorned with excellent moral instruction, adapted both for the guidance of our active and contemplative life, and entitled on account of its inspired authors, to be regarded as a work of extreme piety and goodness.

The above quotations are worthy of consideration. Let those Jews then, who would attempt to cast a slur upon the Talmud, look for one moment at these remarks, and pause while reflecting, that they were made by Catholics, ere they proceed in their attacks upon a work which could command such expressions from those whose religion was so widely different, but whose reason could not refuse to yield to the cogent proofs the divine book in itself contained.

FOOTNOTES:

[A] See the end of the book for an explanation of the Jewish months and years.

OF THE JEWISH MONTHS AND YEARS.

Time is the duration of things; it is divided into years, months, weeks, days, hours, minutes, and seconds. A year is the space of twelve months, which is the time the sun takes in passing through the twelve signs of the Zodiac. The Zodiac is a circle showing the earth's yearly path through the heavens. On this circle are marked the twelve signs, which are numbers of stars, reduced by the fancy of men into the form of animals, and from these forms they take their name. A month is the time the moon occupies in going round the earth. There are two kinds of months, Lunar and Solar. Lunar months are calculated by the moon; solar months are reckoned by the sun. The Hebrews make use of lunar months which consist alternately of twenty-nine and thirty days. The sacred volume directs them to make their computations by lunar months. The plan adopted by them at this day is that which was so admirably arranged by the celebrated and learned Rabbi Hillel, the Prince. The difference between the solar and the lunar months would occasion, in a period of seventeen years, the passover to occur in the autumn month called Tishree, instead of Neson, the spring month; and thus the feast of tabernacles would be in Neson instead of Tishree. To avoid such imperfections in their calculations, the Rabbins have arranged that every third year shall consist of thirteen lunar months instead of twelve. This additional month is called an intercalary month, and the year in which it occurs is called leap year. By this arrangement it will be found that, in the course of nineteen years, there are seven leap years, as follow:

The third, sixth, eighth, eleventh, fourteenth, seventeenth, and nineteenth. The moon was more regarded by the Jews than the sun, because by the new moon all their festivals and fasts were regulated. The new moon was always the beginning of the month. Persons were appointed to watch its first appearance and represent the same to the Sanhedrin, who immediately made it known to the whole of the nation. The new moon was celebrated by the sound of trumpets, and an extra sacrifice was offered in the holy temple.

The ancient Jews had originally no particular names for their months. It is found occasionally in the Bible that names were given to some of the months. These names were made use of as descriptive of the season in which such month occurred; as we find by Moses the legislator, who called the name of the first month Abib, it being the spring time of the year. The present names of the Hebrew months are Chaldaic, and are said to have first been made use of by the nation during the captivity of Babylon. History informs us that these names were used both by the Chaldeans and the Persians. The Jews always reckon their day from evening to evening, because, in the account of the creation of the world the evening is mentioned before the morning; and thus it is that the Sabbaths, festivals and fasts commence from the previous evening. They have no particular names in Hebrew for the days of the week; they are called first, second, third, fourth, fifth, sixth, and the seventh is called *Sabbath*.

The term week owes its derivation to the Hebrew word *Shovuang*, which signifies seventh, on which day God rested from his labors. In former times the Jews had three sorts of weeks:

First—Weeks of Days, which were reckoned from Sabbath to Sabbath. Second—Weeks of Years, which were reckoned from one sabbatical year to another. The sabbatical year happened every seventh year. This year was called *Shemittah*, or year of release. Third—Weeks of seven times seven years, or forty-nine years, and the fiftieth year was called the year of *Youvile*, or Jubilee. The Jubilee was celebrated on the day of atonement, and was proclaimed by the sounding of rams' horns and seven trumpets. The Jubilee allowed the same privileges as the sabbatical year. On both these occasions the ground was not cultivated, but suffered to lie at rest, in order to recruit its fruitful powers. All Hebrew slaves were set at liberty, and all lands or houses, that may have been sold or pledged, returned to the original owners.

It is thus plainly shown that the sabbatical year was evidently appointed to inculcate humanity, fellow-feeling, and brotherly love. At these periods the sovereignty of the Almighty was publicly acknowledged by the restoration of all property to its original and proper owner! Brotherly love was exercised by setting at liberty all bondsmen: thus showing that all men are equal in the eyes of the the Lord; and humanity was promoted by the care which was taken of the poor and the stranger.

PRAYER IN BEHALF OF THE UNITED STATES OF AMERICA.

The following prayer is read in the Synagogue in Lodge street, Cincinnati, on Sabbaths and festivals, the same having been composed by the Rev. H. A. Henry, Minister of the said Synagogue, at the request of the Board of Trustees of the congregation, as a substitute for the Hebrew prayer formerly used by them, in accordance with the custom and practice of the various European congregations.

PRAYER.

Almighty God and Supreme Governor of the Universe. Thou who art enthroned on high, and condescendest to look down, on earth, O! bless and prosper in thine abundant goodness, this *happy* country—this land of *freedom*—which thou hast destined to be our resting-place—*the United States of America*. Grant, O Lord, that virtue, truth, charity and mercy may flourish in these States. O! bless the inhabitants of this land! Grant that nought but peace and happiness may surround them both at home and abroad. Deliver them from all dangers and misfortunes! Endue them with the spirit of love and affection for each other, that they may live as brethren, as the children of the Universal Father of all mankind for ever and ever.

Pour forth, O Lord, thy blessings toward their excellencies the President and the Vice-President of the United States. May they be favored with health and vigor, and may all their efforts for the well-doing of the people prove prosperous. May righteousness and justice flourish in their days. O! banish all errors from their minds, and fashion their hearts according to thy infinite and gracious providence.

O! shed thy grace, O God, upon the Governor of this State, and the Mayor and Common Council of this City. Teach them to judge the people truly. Instruct them in the path they should tread, that their administration may prove wise, steady and prosperous.

Send forth thy salvation, O Lord, into this City, and unto all its inhabitants. O! spread over them thy pavillion of peace, and remove from them all sorrows—all troubles—protect them and shield them from all harm. Incline their hearts unto wisdom and piety, that they may serve thee in holiness of life and purity of soul.

And we, thy chosen people, Israel! O! satisfy us with thy goodness! Let us also rejoice in thy salvation! Guide us, O Lord, by thy unerring Providence, that we may find grace in thy sight, and favor in the eyes of the world. O may our daily supplications ascend thy throne of Grace, that we may live in peace with all mankind, and seek the welfare of the land where thou in thy mercy hast directed our course. In their days, and in our days, may Judah be saved, Israel dwell in comfort, and the Redeemer come unto Zion! O! may such be thy Divine Will, and let us say—Amen.

www.ingramcontent.com/pod-product-compliance
Ingram Content Group UK Ltd.
Pitfield, Milton Keynes, MK11 3LW, UK
UKHW031835270325
456796UK00003B/421